easygourmet

Great American Opportunities Inc.

President: Thomas F. McDow III
Managing Editor: Mary Cummings
Project Manager: Ashlee Brown
Creative and Product Manager: Karen Bird
Editors: Linda Bennie, Georgia Brazil, Linda Jones,
Carolyn King, Debbie Van Mol, Joy Wilson
Art Director: Steve Newman
Book Design: Bill Kersey
Typographers: Jessie Anglin, Sara Anglin
Essayist: Carolyn King
Production Manager: Mark Sloan
Senior Manufacturing Coordinator: George McAllister

Cover Design: Tal Howell Design
Photographs: Flyleaf and pages 69, and 104, Thomas J. Lipton;
Reverse of flyleaf and page 103, The Sugar Association;
Pages 35 and 36, National Turkey Federation;
Page 70, American Spice Trade Association

Easy Gourmet
is a collection of our favorite recipes,
which are not necessarily original recipes.

Published by
Great American Opportunities Inc.
P.O. Box 305142
Nashville, Tennessee 37230

ISBN: 0-87197-822-9

Manufactured in the United States of America
First Printing 1997 75,000 copies

CONTENTS

A Guide to *Easy Gourmet*

Easy Gourmet: at first glance this appears to be an oxymoron—a combination of contradictory words. When you think gourmet, you likely think of recipes with unusual, new ingredients that are to be found in upscale restaurants. When you think easy, you're probably thinking quick-to-fix with accessible ingredients.

To reconcile the two, we've taken classic recipes and modified the haute cuisine to accommodate the food connoisseur who is looking for ways to save time. The result is dishes that taste the same as the more-involved versions but are easy to prepare.

So what are the changes involved? Do-ahead recipes are a major time saver in which all or parts of the food may be prepared and stored, such as salsas or won ton cups. Or choose from an array of make-ahead desserts, such as an ice cream bombe that keeps in the freezer, or a fondue you can freeze and then microwave to serve with fresh fruit and cubes of cake.

You will notice few international recipes because the trend is toward the new American cuisine, with its emphasis on more fresh vegetables and pasta main dishes. You'll probably find all the ingredients for your chosen recipes at your local market. Those hard-to-find specialty-store components have been converted to items readily available. And you'll have no need to go gourmandering to a cookery shop in search of moulds, timbales, or a bain-marie. A minimal set of cookware will suffice.

Easy Gourmet is divided into several categories that make up four chapters, from which you're sure to find just the right selection for any food occasion. To help you make your menu selections at a glance, we've provided a table of contents after each chapter introduction that contains all the recipe titles in the chapter. Even the titles are an invitation to try these recipes.

Try starting at the beginning of the book: whether you plan to use the recipes as the launch of a formal dinner or as a mini meal in themselves, look through the appetizers. There's Bleu Cheese Puffs, Brie Crowned with Sun-Dried Tomatoes, or Stuffed Fresh Snow Peas, for example. They lead into the Soups, with such savory possibilities as Sweet Potato Vichyssoise. From there, select a bread from a tempting variety that includes everything from Old Country Scones to Tomato-Cheese Braids, Green Tomato Bread Loaves to Molasses Bran Muffins with Raisins.

A salad might include artichokes or squash and pasta, or Lettuce Stuffed with Cheese and Vegetables. The choice is yours, and here, as with all our recipes, the choice also is yours as to how much time you wish to spend on the recipe. A quick scan lets you see the amount of preparation involved so you can gauge your time accordingly.

From our vegetables and side dishes, just decide your preference and turn to it. Then see all the different ways to present the dish: will you serve potatoes as croquettes or as wedges smothered in Parmesan? Will it be Texas-style rice or Chinese rice stir-fried? As you continue into Main Dishes, you'll have regional as well as continental from which to select: Cajun, Southwestern, Italian, Jamaican, West Indian, and more.

As complex or simple as you want, as caloric or light as you choose, the desserts include fondue, cake, meringue, charlotte, and pie, among others. With enigmatic titles such as Gateau au Chocolat, Raisin Mumbles, or Valentine Stained Glass Hearts, you may decide to try a recipe just to be surprised by the result. Other recipe names sound as if they're just the selection to list at the end of a gourmet menu: an Olde English Raspberry Trifle, Poached Pears in Red Currant Jelly, or Frango Mint Bombe.

Don't overlook the beverage section, where you'll find refreshing floats, coolers, ciders, and mocha mix. Another seemingly contradictory term—light refreshment—comes in the form of flavored coffees, which are often served instead of heavy desserts.

An additional way we've made your work easier is by the inclusion of charts. They're a quick reference guide as well as a source of ideas when you need them fast. Dessert Ideas gives hints for creating really quick desserts, for creating an elegant look, for cutting calories, and for different kinds of toppings, as well as serving ideas and preparation tips. Did you know, for example, that whipped cream is fluffier and less likely to separate if you use confectioners' sugar instead of granulated?

A chart of Equivalents helps you convert that four-ounce can of mushrooms, for which you want to substitute fresh, into measurable terms. Do you sometimes agonize over how many slices of bread you need to provide a cup of dried bread crumbs, or just how many ounces of cheese you need to purchase if the recipe calls for a cup of shredded cheese? Thumb over to the chart for an immediate answer.

An Herbs chart lists major herbs along with the dishes in which they most often are used, and tells you how to preserve fresh herbs. It gives you information you may never have known—saffron is made from the dried stamens of the crocus—and substitutions you may never have considered—no need to cry over the onions when you can use chives instead.

So be as elaborate as you want with the billowing tablecloth, candles, floral arrangement, and mood-setting music. Use the company china. Cut flat fish shapes from carrot rounds to float on your favorite clear soup, or refer to another chart included to help you quickly add a dimension of food decor—a chart on Garnishes. These suggestions, easily incorporated with any part of your meal, include clear and easy instructions. Use them in whole or as a base on which to add your own creative innovations. You'll have the time to present a classic setting with the time you saved by cooking easy gourmet. On second glance, there's really no longer a conflict in terms.

appetizers soups breads

Appetizers • Soups • Breads

Bleu Cheese Puffs

4 ounces bleu cheese

3 ounces cream cheese, softened

2 tablespoons butter, softened

1 to 2 tablespoons heavy cream

1/2 cup chopped pecans

24 Miniature Cream Puffs for Hors d'Oeuvre (page 21)

Blend the bleu cheese, cream cheese, butter and cream in a bowl. Stir in the pecans. Spoon into the cream puff shells; replace the tops. Chill, wrapped in foil, until serving time. May be frozen.

Yield: 24 servings.

Miniature Swiss Quiche Squares

1 (8-count) can crescent dinner rolls

4 long slices Swiss cheese

3 eggs, lightly beaten

1 tablespoon finely chopped onion

3/4 cup milk

4 slices bacon, crisp-cooked, crumbled

1 tablespoon chopped fresh parsley

Separate the roll dough into 4 rectangles. Press 2 rectangles over the bottom and 1 inch up the sides of 2 oiled and floured 8x8-inch baking pans; seal the edges and perforations. Layer the cheese slices over the dough. Combine the eggs, onion and milk in a bowl; whisk until smooth. Pour into the prepared pans. Sprinkle with the bacon and parsley. Bake at 425 degrees for 15 to 18 minutes or until set. Cool for 5 minutes. Cut into squares.

Yield: 32 servings.

Baked Brie on French Sourdough

2 French sourdough rolls

Margarine

1/2 cup packed brown sugar

1/4 cup chopped almonds

15 ounces Brie cheese, sliced

Cut the round ends from the rolls and discard. Cut each roll into four 1/2-inch slices. Spread margarine over 1 side of the bread. Combine the brown sugar and almonds in a bowl. Layer each slice of bread with the almond mixture and a slice of Brie cheese. Place on an ungreased baking sheet. Bake at 375 degrees for 6 to 7 minutes or until heated through. Serve with dry white wine.

Yield: 8 servings.

Brie Crowned with Sun-Dried Tomatoes

15 ounces Brie cheese

2 cloves of garlic, minced

2 1/2 tablespoons minced fresh parsley

2 1/2 tablespoons freshly grated Parmesan cheese

5 sun-dried tomatoes, minced

2 tablespoons minced fresh basil

1 tablespoon vegetable oil

Remove the rind from the Brie cheese and place the Brie on a serving platter. Mash the garlic in a bowl to a paste consistency. Stir in the parsley, Parmesan cheese, sun-dried tomatoes, basil and oil. Spread evenly over the top of the Brie. Let stand at room temperature for 1 hour. Serve with assorted party crackers or toasted French bread slices.

Yield: 6 servings.

Dates Wrapped in Cheese Pastry

8 ounces Cheddar cheese, shredded

1/2 cup margarine

1 1/4 cups sifted flour

1/2 teaspoon cayenne pepper

15 pitted dates

15 pecan halves

Let the cheese and margarine stand in a bowl at room temperature until softened. Cut in the flour and pepper as for pie dough. Slit the dates; stuff with the pecan halves. Flatten a small amount of dough in the palm of the hand. Wrap a date in the dough, sealing completely. Repeat with the remaining dough and dates. Place on a baking sheet. Bake at 400 degrees for 15 minutes or until light brown. Store between sheets of waxed paper in an airtight container.

Yield: 15 servings.

Antipasto

2 small jars marinated artichokes, chopped

2 pints marinated mushrooms

1 jar pepper salad

2 cans pitted black olives, drained

1 can chick-peas, drained

1 small link pepperoni, thinly sliced

1 jar stuffed large hot peppers, drained

2 jars Tuscan peppers, drained

1 jar cauliflower, drained

Oregano to taste

4 (1/2-inch-thick) slices Genoa salami, cubed

4 (1/2-inch-thick) slices Provolone cheese, cubed

1 or 2 pints cherry tomatoes

1 can anchovies (optional)

Parmesan Rounds (page 21)

Combine the artichokes, mushrooms and undrained pepper salad in a large bowl. Add the olives, chick-peas, pepperoni, hot peppers, Tuscan peppers, cauliflower and oregano in a large bowl. Chill, covered, for 8 to 10 hours or up to several days. Add the salami, cheese, tomatoes and anchovies; mix gently. Serve with Parmesan Rounds.

Yield: 15 servings.

Baked Artichoke Cheese Dip

1 cup mayonnaise

1 cup shredded mozzarella cheese

1 cup grated Parmesan cheese

1 (16-ounce) can artichoke hearts, finely chopped

Combine the mayonnaise, mozzarella cheese, Parmesan cheese and artichoke hearts in a bowl; mix well. Pour into a greased 8x8-inch baking dish. Bake at 350 degrees for 15 to 20 minutes or until bubbly. Serve warm with crackers or chips.

Yield: 30 servings.

Sautéed Eggplant with Tomato Vinaigrette

3 cups chopped peeled eggplant

1/3 cup chopped green bell pepper

1 onion, chopped

2 cloves of garlic, crushed

1/3 cup olive oil

1/2 cup chopped mushrooms

1 can tomato paste

1/4 cup water

2 tablespoons red wine vinegar

1/2 cup sliced Spanish olives

1 1/2 teaspoons sugar

1/2 teaspoon oregano

1/8 teaspoon pepper

1 teaspoon salt

Sauté the eggplant, green pepper, onion and garlic in hot olive oil in a skillet for 10 minutes or until golden brown. Stir in a mixture of the mushrooms, tomato paste and water. Add the remaining ingredients. Simmer, covered, for 30 minutes or until the eggplant is tender, stirring occasionally. Chill, covered, for 8 to 10 hours. Serve hot or cold with crackers.

Yield: 12 servings.

Baked Mushrooms with Garlic Butter

8 ounces cream cheese, softened

1 cup sour cream

1 cup mayonnaise

1 bunch green onions, chopped

1/4 cup crumbled crisp-cooked bacon

1/2 tablespoon lemon juice

1/2 tablespoon seasoned salt

60 medium mushrooms

4 ounces Cheddar cheese, sliced

1/4 cup melted garlic butter

Process the cream cheese, sour cream and mayonnaise in a blender until creamy. Add the green onions, crumbled bacon, lemon juice and seasoned salt; mix well. Remove the mushroom stems and discard. Fill the mushroom caps with the cream cheese mixture. Cut the Cheddar cheese slices into squares; cover the filling in the mushrooms with the cheese. Place in a baking dish. Drizzle with the garlic butter. Bake at 425 degrees for 10 minutes or until the mushrooms are tender.

Yield: 60 servings.

Mushrooms with Crab and Smoked Salmon

3 cups sliced fresh shiitake mushrooms

2 tablespoons chopped shallots

1 tablespoon soy sauce

3 tablespoons butter   2 cups heavy cream

1 1/2 pounds cream cheese, softened

8 ounces jumbo lump crab meat

1/4 cup butter, softened

120 bread rounds, plain or toasted, or cucumber slices

1/2 pound smoked salmon, thinly sliced

3 tablespoons chopped fresh dill

Sauté the mushrooms and shallots with the soy sauce in 3 tablespoons butter in a skillet until the mushrooms are soft. Add the cream to the skillet and simmer until reduced by half. Remove the skillet from the heat and let the mushroom mixture cool. Beat the cream cheese in a mixing bowl until smooth. Fold in the crab meat and mushroom mixture. Chill for 1 hour. Spread the bread rounds or cucumber slices with 1/4 cup softened butter and top with 1/2 tablespoon of the mushroom mixture. Wrap or top the canapés with the smoked salmon and sprinkle with the dill. Grated cucumber may be used to garnish the canapés.

Yield: 120 servings.

Stuffed Fresh Snow Peas

3 ounces cream cheese, softened

1½ tablespoons catsup

3 tablespoons chopped green bell pepper

2 tablespoons finely chopped onion

1½ tablespoons chopped pimento

⅓ cup finely chopped pecans

¼ teaspoon salt

¼ teaspoon pepper

30 tender fresh snow peas

Combine the cream cheese, catsup, green pepper, onion, pimento, pecans, salt and pepper in a bowl; mix well. Chill for 1 hour or longer. String the snow peas. Blanch in boiling water in a saucepan for 30 seconds. Plunge into cold water; drain. Slit the straight side of each snow pea to open. Stuff each with 1½ teaspoons cream cheese filling. Chill, covered, until serving time.

Yield: 30 servings.

Parmesan Spinach Balls

2 (10-ounce) packages frozen chopped spinach, thawed, drained

2 cups herb-seasoned stuffing mix

2 medium onions, chopped

½ cup sliced celery or water chestnuts

6 eggs, beaten

¾ cup melted butter

½ cup grated Parmesan cheese

1 teaspoon garlic salt

½ teaspoon pepper

½ teaspoon thyme

Dash of Tabasco sauce

Combine the spinach, stuffing mix, onions, celery, eggs, butter, cheese, garlic salt, pepper, thyme and Tabasco in a bowl; mix well. Chill in the refrigerator for 2 hours. Shape into 1½-inch balls; place in a baking dish. Bake at 350 degrees for 20 minutes.

Yield: 60 servings.

Baked Crab with Cream Cheese and Almonds

16 ounces cream cheese, softened

1/3 cup mayonnaise

1 tablespoon confectioners' sugar

1 tablespoon chablis

1/2 teaspoon prepared mustard

1/4 teaspoon onion powder

1/4 teaspoon garlic salt

1/4 teaspoon salt

12 ounces fresh crab meat, drained, flaked

1/4 teaspoon paprika

1/3 cup sliced almonds, toasted

Combine the cream cheese, mayonnaise, confectioners' sugar, chablis, mustard, onion powder, garlic salt and salt in a bowl. Stir in the crab meat. Spoon into a lightly greased 1-quart baking dish. Sprinkle with the paprika and almonds. Bake at 375 degrees for 15 minutes or until hot and bubbly.

Yield: 12 servings.

Oriental Lobster Wrapped in Bacon

12 ounces lobster

1/3 cup fine soft bread crumbs

2 tablespoons soy sauce

1 teaspoon chopped chives

1 teaspoon lemon juice

1 teaspoon dry mustard

Dillweed to taste

1/4 teaspoon salt

10 slices bacon, cut into thirds

Chop the lobster. Combine with the bread crumbs, soy sauce, chives, lemon juice, dry mustard, dillweed and salt in a bowl; mix well. Chill for 30 minutes. Shape by tablespoonfuls into 30 rolls. Wrap each with a bacon piece; secure with a wooden pick. Place on a rack in a broiler pan. Broil for 12 minutes or until the bacon is crisp.

Yield: 30 servings.

Smoked Salmon Bruschetta

1 clove of garlic, minced

3 to 4 ounces smoked salmon, chopped

4 ounces mozzarella cheese, shredded

1 tomato, chopped

3 ounces toasted pine nuts

2 to 3 tablespoons extra-virgin olive oil

Fresh basil, chopped

8 (1/4-inch) slices French baguette, toasted

Combine the garlic, salmon and cheese in bowl. Add the tomato, pine nuts, olive oil and basil; mix well. Serve with toasted baguette.

Yield: 8 servings.

Smoked Salmon Canapés

1/2 cup butter, softened

10 thin slices white bread

Freshly ground pepper to taste

1/2 pound smoked salmon, thinly sliced

Spread the butter on the bread slices and sprinkle with the pepper. Cover with the salmon slices. Cut with cookie cutters into desired shapes. Chill, covered tightly with plastic wrap.

Yield: 40 servings.

Rumaki Polynesian

1 pound bacon

2 (7-ounce) cans whole water chestnuts, drained

1 (14-ounce) bottle catsup

1 teaspoon Worcestershire sauce

Soy sauce and hot sauce to taste

1/2 to 1 cup sugar

Cut the bacon slices into halves. Wrap the water chestnuts with the bacon pieces; secure with wooden picks. Place in a shallow 9x13-inch baking dish. Bake at 350 degrees for 30 minutes; drain. Combine the catsup, Worcestershire sauce, soy sauce, hot sauce and sugar in a bowl; mix well. Pour over the water chestnuts. Bake for 30 minutes longer.

Yield: 20 servings.

Garlic Shrimp in Won Ton Cups

12 won ton wraps

1 pound cooked shrimp, chopped

3 cloves of garlic, minced

2 tablespoons chopped water chestnuts

1/4 cup finely chopped seeded cucumber

3 green onions, finely chopped

2 tablespoons capers

3 tablespoons olive oil

1 1/2 teaspoons lemon juice

1/2 teaspoon Dijon mustard

Salt, red pepper and fresh dill to taste

Spray 12 medium muffin cups or 24 miniature muffin cups with nonstick baking spray. Press the won ton wraps into the muffin cups to form shells. Bake at 375 degrees for 5 to 7 minutes or until brown. Let stand until cool. Combine the shrimp, garlic, water chestnuts, cucumber, green onions, capers, olive oil, lemon juice, Dijon mustard, salt, red pepper and dill in a bowl; mix well. Chill, covered, until serving time. Spoon the shrimp mixture into the baked shells just before serving. Arrange on a serving platter.

Yield: 12 servings.

Vegetable Seafood Won Tons

1 envelope Lipton vegetable recipe soup mix

15 ounces low-fat ricotta cheese

8 ounces imitation crab meat or 1 1/2 cups cooked shrimp, chopped

1/4 teaspoon garlic powder

1/8 teaspoon pepper

40 won ton wrappers

1 tablespoon water

1 tablespoon olive oil or vegetable oil

10 green onion tops

Combine the soup mix, ricotta cheese, imitation crab meat, garlic powder and pepper in a bowl and mix well. Place 1 tablespoonful of the mixture in the center of each won ton wrapper. Brush the edges with water. Bring up the corners to enclose the filling; press to seal. Place seam side down on a lightly greased baking sheet; brush with oil. Bake at 350 degrees for 25 minutes or until crisp and golden brown, turning once. Cut each onion top into 4 slivers. Tie 1 sliver around each won ton.

Yield: 40 servings.

Photograph for this recipe is on the flyleaf.

Exceptional Paté

½ cup chopped onion

3 tablespoons butter

1 small tart apple, peeled, chopped

3 tablespoons butter

1 pound chicken livers

2 tablespoons whipping cream

2 tablespoons butter, softened

Salt, pepper and chili powder to taste

Sauté the onion in the 3 tablespoons butter in a skillet until translucent. Add the apple. Cook until the apple is soft, stirring frequently. Remove to a food processor container. Melt 3 tablespoons butter in a skillet. Add the chicken livers. Cook until brown but still pink inside, stirring frequently. Add the chicken livers and cream to the food processor container. Process until creamy and smooth, adding additional cream if necessary for desired consistency. Stir 2 tablespoons butter into the paté. Add the salt, pepper and chili powder; mix well. Spoon into a serving dish. Chill, covered, before serving. May be stored in the refrigerator for up to 2 days or frozen. Serve with crackers.

Yield: 48 servings.

Dilled Mustard Cream Cheese with Ham on Toast

8 slices white bread

8 ounces thinly sliced baked ham

¼ cup unsalted butter, softened

3 ounces cream cheese, softened

1 teaspoon minced fresh dillweed

½ teaspoon dry mustard

Trim the crusts from the bread and cut the bread into halves diagonally. Place on a baking sheet. Broil until toasted. Reserve 1 slice ham. Combine the remaining ham with the butter, cream cheese, dillweed and dry mustard in a food processor container; process until puréed. Spread on the toast triangles. Cut reserved ham into small pieces. Place on each triangle; garnish with a sprig of dillweed.

Yield: 16 servings.

Miniature Cream Puffs for Hors d'Oeuvre

1 cup water
1/2 cup butter or margarine
1 cup flour
1/4 teaspoon salt
4 eggs

Heat the water and butter to a rolling boil in a saucepan. Stir in the flour and salt. Cook over low heat for 1 minute or until the mixture forms a ball, stirring constantly. Remove from the heat. Cool slightly. Beat in the eggs 1 at a time. Drop by rounded teaspoonfuls onto an ungreased baking sheet. Bake at 400 degrees for 25 minutes or until puffed and golden brown. Cool on wire racks. Cut off tops. Remove soft dough. Fill with chicken or tuna salad; replace the tops.

Yield: 60 servings.

Parmesan Rounds

1 (16-ounce) loaf sliced bread
1/3 cup butter, softened
8 ounces cream cheese, softened
1/4 cup mayonnaise
2 green onions, finely chopped
1/2 cup grated Parmesan cheese
Garlic powder to taste

Cut the bread into rounds with a cookie cutter. Spread lightly with some of the butter. Place on a baking sheet. Broil until lightly toasted on both sides. Combine the remaining butter with the cream cheese, mayonnaise, green onions, cheese and garlic powder in a bowl; mix well. Spread on toasted bread. Broil until bubbly.

Yield: 24 servings.

Chilled Avocado Soup

2 medium avocados 1½ cups water

1 cup milk 2 tablespoons lemon juice

2½ teaspoons seasoned salt

Dash of red pepper sauce

1 medium tomato, chopped 8 lemon slices

Slice the avocados lengthwise into fourths. Press through a sieve into a mixer bowl. Add the water, milk and lemon juice gradually, beating until the mixture is smooth. Stir in the seasoned salt, pepper sauce and tomato. Chill, covered, in the refrigerator. Spoon into soup bowls. Top with the lemon slices.

Yield: 8 servings.

Fresh Strawberry Soup

2 cups cold strawberries

1 cup low-fat buttermilk

1 tablespoon plus 1 teaspoon sugar

Combine the strawberries, buttermilk and sugar in a blender container. Process until the strawberries are puréed. Serve immediately or chill in the refrigerator.

Yield: 4 servings.

Photograph for this recipe is on the reverse of the flyleaf.

Chicken and Wild Rice Soup

2 whole boneless skinless chicken breasts

¾ cup uncooked wild rice

¾ cup uncooked brown or white rice

1 stalk celery, chopped

1 small onion, chopped

1 tablespoon chopped parsley

2 chicken bouillon cubes

1 bay leaf

¼ teaspoon celery seeds

1 teaspoon salt

½ teaspoon celery salt

½ teaspoon seasoned salt

2 cups milk

1 cup half-and-half

Rinse the chicken. Cook in water to cover in a heavy 6-quart saucepan until tender. Remove the chicken, reserving about 1 quart broth in saucepan. Cool the chicken. Chop into bite-size pieces. Return to the broth with the rice, celery, onion, parsley, bouillon cubes, bay leaf, celery seeds, salt, celery salt and seasoned salt; mix well. Simmer until the rice is tender. Stir in the milk and half-and-half. Cook just until heated through. Do not boil. Discard the bay leaf.

Yield: 6 servings.

Savory Chicken Noodle Soup

1 cup uncooked fine egg noodles
1 tablespoon dried minced onion
2 1/2 tablespoons chicken bouillon granules
1 teaspoon pepper
1/4 teaspoon dried whole thyme
1/8 teaspoon celery seeds
1/8 teaspoon garlic powder
1 bay leaf
8 cups water
1 carrot, finely chopped
3 cups chopped cooked chicken

Combine the egg noodles, minced onion, chicken bouillon, pepper, thyme, celery seeds, garlic powder, bay leaf, water and carrot in a saucepan. Bring to a boil. Reduce the heat; simmer for 15 minutes, stirring occasionally. Discard the bay leaf. Stir in the chicken. Simmer for 5 minutes longer, stirring occasionally.

Yield: 8 servings.

Indian Corn Soup

1 (16-ounce) can navy beans
3 (14-ounce) cans chicken broth
3 (4-ounce) cans chopped green chiles
1 large onion, chopped
1/2 bunch fresh cilantro, chopped
3 (16-ounce) cans white hominy
1 tablespoon cumin
1 tablespoon ground oregano
1/2 teaspoon ground red pepper
3 large cloves of garlic, crushed
1/2 teaspoon black pepper
2 tablespoons butter or margarine
3 slices bacon, chopped
4 cups chopped cooked chicken breasts
1 cup shredded Cheddar cheese
1/4 cup flour

Combine the beans with liquid, chicken broth, chiles, onion, cilantro, hominy, cumin, oregano, red pepper, garlic, black pepper, butter, bacon and chicken in a 6-quart stockpot; mix well. Simmer for 3 hours, stirring occasionally. Add the cheese, stirring until melted. Mix the flour with enough water to blend in a small bowl. Stir into the soup. Cook for 10 minutes or until thickened, stirring constantly. Serve with corn tortillas or corn chips.

Yield: 10 servings.

Chilled Yellow Pepper Soup

2 medium carrots, chopped
1 large onion, chopped
1 tablespoon margarine
1¼ cups chicken broth
1 yellow bell pepper, chopped
½ teaspoon salt
3 ounces cream cheese, softened
Red pepper and nutmeg to taste
½ cup milk ½ cup sour cream
1 to 2 tablespoons milk

Sauté the carrots and onion in the margarine in a large saucepan for 10 minutes or until tender. Stir in the chicken broth. Bring to a boil over medium-high heat. Add the yellow pepper; reduce the heat. Simmer, covered, for 15 minutes or until the pepper is tender. Cool slightly. Add the salt, cream cheese, red pepper and nutmeg; stir until the cream cheese melts. Process in a blender until smooth. Chill, covered, for 4 hours to 4 days. Blend ½ cup milk into soup. Ladle into soup bowls. Blend the sour cream with enough milk to thin to desired consistency. Drizzle a circle over the surface of the soup; cut with a knife to make spokes in the manner of a spider web. Serve immediately.

Yield: 4 servings.

Creamy Carrot Soup

3 cups water
1 bouillon cube
4 cups sliced carrots
1 Golden Delicious apple, peeled, cubed
2 tablespoons brown sugar
Cinnamon to taste
2 teaspoons curry powder
2 tablespoons low-fat plain yogurt
Fresh chives

Combine the water and bouillon cube in a large saucepan. Bring to a boil over medium heat, stirring until the bouillon cube is dissolved. Remove from the heat. Steam the carrots and apple in a vegetable steamer or saucepan for 15 minutes or until very tender. Process with the bouillon in several batches in a blender until puréed. Pour into a large container. Add the sugar, cinnamon and curry powder; mix well. Chill, covered, for 1 hour or longer. Pour into soup bowls and add a dollop of yogurt. Garnish with chives.

Yield: 6 servings.

Photograph for this recipe is on the reverse of the flyleaf.

Sour Cream Potato Chowder

3 cups diced potatoes

1/2 cup finely chopped celery

1/2 cup finely chopped onion

3 cups water

2 cups scalded milk

2 chicken bouillon cubes

3 tablespoons butter

1 cup sour cream

1 tablespoon flour

Salt and pepper to taste

Combine the potatoes, celery, onion and water in a medium saucepan. Cook, covered, until the potatoes are tender, stirring occasionally. Add the milk, bouillon cubes and butter. Combine the sour cream and flour in a small bowl; mix until smooth. Add to the soup mixture. Cook until the bouillon cubes are dissolved and the chowder is thickened, stirring constantly. Stir in the salt and pepper.

Yield: 6 servings.

Sweet Potato Vichyssoise

1 3/4 cups sliced green onions

5 cups chicken broth

2 1/2 pounds sweet potatoes, baked

Salt and pepper to taste

1/2 cup half-and-half

Chopped chives to taste

Combine the green onions and 1 cup of the chicken broth in a large saucepan and simmer for 15 minutes or until the green onions are tender. Scoop the pulp from the sweet potatoes. Discard the skins. Purée the sweet potato pulp with the green onion mixture in a blender container until puréed. Spoon purée into a saucepan. Add the remaining chicken broth and simmer for 5 minutes. Season with the salt and pepper and remove from the heat. Chill in the refrigerator. Stir the half-and-half into the chilled mixture. Spoon into soup bowls. Garnish with chives. May substitute evaporated skim milk for the half-and-half to reduce fat.

Yield: 8 servings.

Butternut Squash Soup

1 medium butternut squash, chopped
1 cup chopped celery
1 carrot, chopped
1 apple, chopped
6 cups chicken broth
Half-and-half

Combine the squash, celery, carrot and apple with the chicken broth in a saucepan. Cook until the vegetables are tender, stirring occasionally. Process in a blender until puréed. Add enough half-and-half to make of the desired consistency. Cook in a saucepan over medium heat just until heated through.

Yield: 8 servings.

Fresh Vegetable Soup

1 large onion, chopped
1 head cabbage, shredded
6 fresh tomatoes, chopped
1 large green bell pepper, chopped
1 rib celery, chopped
1 (16-ounce) can tomatoes
1 clove of garlic, crushed
Salt and pepper to taste
Grated Parmesan cheese

Combine the onion, cabbage, fresh tomatoes, green pepper, celery, canned tomatoes, garlic, salt and pepper with water to cover in a large saucepan. Simmer for 2½ to 3 hours, stirring occasionally. Ladle into soup bowls. Sprinkle with cheese.

Yield: 8 servings.

Parmesan Croutons

Heat 3 tablespoons butter and 3 tablespoons olive oil in a large skillet over medium-high heat. Add 3 cups of ½-inch bread cubes and sauté over medium-low heat for 10 minutes. Add 2 cloves of minced garlic and 1 teaspoon each of parsley, chives and tarragon. Sauté for 10 minutes longer or until brown and crisp. Toss the croutons with 3 tablespoons Parmesan cheese in a large bowl. Spread on a tray to cool. Store in an airtight container. Serve with soups or salads.

Breadsticks with Rosemary and Chives

1 (10-count) can soft breadsticks

1 egg white, lightly beaten

Salt to taste

1 to 1½ teaspoons dried rosemary

1 to 1½ teaspoons dried chives

Unroll the dough. Separate at the perforations into 10 breadsticks. Twist each breadstick; place on an ungreased baking sheet, pressing down the ends to keep bread twisted. Brush the tops of the breadsticks with the egg white. Season lightly with salt. Sprinkle the rosemary and chives over the top. Bake at 350 degrees for 15 to 18 minutes or until brown.

Yield: 10 servings.

Savory Cheese Biscuits

1 (10-count) can biscuits

⅓ cup melted butter

3 tablespoons crumbled bleu cheese

Cut the biscuits into quarters. Arrange in a 12x13-inch baking dish. Combine the butter and cheese in a bowl; mix well. Pour over the biscuits. Bake at 400 degrees for 15 minutes.

Yield: 40 servings.

Bacon and Vegetable Bread

½ cup melted butter or margarine

⅓ cup grated Parmesan cheese

3 (10-count) cans flaky biscuits, cut into quarters

12 ounces turkey bacon, crisp-cooked, crumbled

½ cup chopped green bell pepper

½ cup chopped onion

Green bell pepper strips

Combine the butter and cheese in a bowl and mix well. Roll the biscuit quarters in the mixture to coat. Arrange ½ of the biscuit quarters in a bundt pan sprayed with nonstick cooking spray. Layer the bacon, chopped green pepper, onion and remaining biscuit quarters ½ at a time over the top. Bake at 350 degrees for 40 minutes or until golden brown. Invert onto a serving plate lined with green pepper strips.

Yield: 8 servings.

Photograph for this recipe is on page 35.

Jalapeño Corn Bread

1 tablespoon vegetable oil

$1\frac{1}{2}$ cups cornmeal mix

1 cup buttermilk

3 tablespoons vegetable oil

1 (8-ounce) can cream-style corn

2 eggs, beaten

Garlic powder to taste

$\frac{1}{2}$ cup chopped green bell pepper

8 slices bacon, crisp-cooked, crumbled

$\frac{1}{2}$ cup canned chopped jalapeño peppers

2 cups shredded sharp Cheddar cheese

Grease a heavy baking pan with 1 tablespoon oil. Preheat the pan in a 350-degree oven for 10 minutes. Combine the cornmeal mix, buttermilk, 3 tablespoons oil, corn, eggs, garlic powder, green pepper, bacon and jalapeño peppers in a bowl; mix well. Pour half the batter into the preheated baking pan. Sprinkle with 1 cup cheese. Top with the remaining batter. Bake at 350 degrees for 45 minutes. Sprinkle with the remaining 1 cup cheese. Bake for 8 to 10 minutes longer or until the cheese melts.

Yield: 10 servings.

Old Country Scones

$\frac{1}{2}$ cup raisins

2 cups flour

3 tablespoons sugar

1 tablespoon baking powder

$\frac{3}{4}$ teaspoon salt

$\frac{1}{2}$ teaspoon baking soda

5 tablespoons butter, softened

1 egg, lightly beaten

1 cup sour cream

1 teaspoon sugar

$\frac{1}{2}$ teaspoon cinnamon

Cover the raisins with hot water in a bowl. Let stand for 5 minutes; drain. Combine the flour, 3 tablespoons sugar, baking powder, salt and baking soda in a bowl. Cut in the butter until crumbly. Add the raisins, egg and sour cream, mixing well after each addition. Knead on a floured surface 10 to 12 times. Place the dough in the center of a greased baking pan. Pat into a $\frac{1}{2}$-inch-thick circle. Cut into 8 wedges. Sprinkle with a mixture of 1 teaspoon sugar and cinnamon. Bake at 425 degrees for 15 to 18 minutes or until light brown. Serve warm.

Yield: 8 servings.

French Herb Bread Knots

2 (10-count) cans soft breadsticks

French Herb Spread

Grated Parmesan cheese to taste

Separate the dough strips and tie each loosely into a knot. Place 1 inch apart on a greased baking sheet. Brush with the French Herb Spread. Sprinkle with the cheese. Bake at 350 degrees for 15 minutes or until golden brown.

Yield: 20 servings.

French Herb Spread

1/2 cup butter, softened

1 teaspoon parsley flakes

1/2 teaspoon oregano

1/2 teaspoon basil

1/2 teaspoon celery seeds

1/8 teaspoon sage

1/8 teaspoon salt

1/4 teaspoon pepper

1 teaspoon grated Parmesan cheese

Combine the butter, parsley flakes, oregano, basil, celery seeds, sage, salt, pepper and cheese in a medium bowl; mix well.

Tomato-Cheese Braids

2 cups biscuit mix

3/4 cup shredded sharp American cheese

2/3 cup tomato juice

Melted butter or margarine

Celery seeds to taste

Combine the biscuit mix and cheese in a bowl. Add the tomato juice all at once, mixing and kneading the dough. Roll into a 6x13-inch rectangle, about 1/2 inch thick. Cut into 1/2x3-inch strips. Shape the strips into braids on an ungreased baking sheet, pressing the ends to keep the dough twisted. Brush with butter. Sprinkle with celery seeds. Bake at 450 degrees for 10 to 15 minutes or until brown.

Yield: 18 servings.

Chive-Garlic Bread Loaf

1/2 cup melted margarine
1/4 cup chopped dried chives
1 teaspoon garlic salt
1 tablespoon Parmesan cheese
3 (10-count) cans biscuits
1 egg yolk, lightly beaten
2 teaspoons water

Combine the margarine, chives, garlic salt and cheese in a bowl; mix well. Reserve 2 biscuits. Brush remaining biscuits generously with the margarine mixture. Grease a 4x15-inch loaf pan. Stand the biscuits in the pan, beginning and ending with a reserved biscuit. Brush with a mixture of the egg yolk and water. Bake at 450 degrees for 15 to 20 minutes or until golden brown. Let stand in pan for 5 minutes. Remove to a napkin-lined basket. Serve warm.

Yield: 30 servings.

Green Tomato Bread Loaves

2/3 cup raisins
2/3 cup boiling water
2/3 cup shortening
2 2/3 cups sugar
4 eggs
2 cups ground green tomatoes
3 1/3 cups flour
2 teaspoons baking soda
1/2 teaspoon baking powder
1 teaspoon ground cloves
1 teaspoon cinnamon
2/3 cup chopped nuts

Soak the raisins in the boiling water. Cream the shortening and sugar in a large mixer bowl. Beat in the eggs one at a time. Add the green tomatoes, raisins and water; beat well. Mix the flour with the baking soda, baking powder, cloves, cinnamon and nuts. Add to the green tomato mixture and mix well. Pour into 2 greased 5x9-inch loaf pans. Sprinkle with additional cinnamon. Bake at 350 degrees for 50 minutes or until a knife inserted near the center comes out clean.

Yield: 24 servings.

Crystal Poppy Seed Bread

3 cups flour

$2\frac{1}{4}$ cups sugar

$\frac{1}{2}$ teaspoon salt

1 teaspoon plus 2 tablespoons baking powder

1 cup plus 2 tablespoons vegetable oil

3 eggs

$1\frac{1}{2}$ cups milk

$1\frac{1}{2}$ teaspoons vanilla extract

1 teaspoon butter flavoring

$1\frac{1}{2}$ tablespoons poppy seeds

$\frac{1}{4}$ cup plus 2 tablespoons orange juice

1 cup plus 2 tablespoons sugar

$\frac{3}{4}$ teaspoon each vanilla, butter and almond flavorings

Combine the flour, $2\frac{1}{4}$ cups sugar, salt and baking powder in a mixer bowl. Add the next 6 ingredients, mixing well. Pour into 2 nonstick 5x9-inch loaf pans. Bake at 350 degrees for 1 hour or until a wooden pick inserted near the center comes out clean. Bring the orange juice, 1 cup plus 2 tablespoons sugar and $\frac{3}{4}$ teaspoon each vanilla, butter and almond flavorings to a boil in a saucepan. Remove from the heat. Pour over hot loaves in the pans. Let stand until sugar crystals form around the edges. Remove to a wire rack to cool.

Yield: 24 servings.

Pineapple Coconut Loaves

1 cup butter, softened

2 cups sugar

4 eggs

1 cup mashed bananas

4 cups flour

2 teaspoons baking powder

1 teaspoon baking soda

$\frac{3}{4}$ teaspoon salt

1 (20-ounce) can crushed pineapple

1 cup flaked coconut

Beat the butter in a mixer bowl until creamy. Add the sugar gradually, beating until light and fluffy. Beat in the eggs 1 at a time. Stir in the bananas. Add a mixture of the flour, baking powder, baking soda and salt, beating just until moistened. Fold in the undrained pineapple and coconut. Spoon into 2 greased and floured 5x9-inch loaf pans. Bake at 350 degrees for 60 to 70 minutes or until the loaves test done. Cool on wire racks.

Yield: 24 servings.

Cottage Cheese Sweet Rolls

1/2 cup heavy cream
1 cup packed light brown sugar
1/4 cup chopped pecans
1 3/4 cups flour
1/8 teaspoon salt
1 1/2 teaspoons baking powder
1/8 teaspoon baking soda
1/4 cup sugar
1 cup cottage cheese
1 egg
1/4 cup margarine, softened
1/4 cup sugar
1 teaspoon cinnamon

Mix the heavy cream, brown sugar and pecans in a bowl. Pour into a greased 9-inch round baking pan. Mix the next 5 ingredients in a bowl. Add the cottage cheese and egg; mix well. Shape into a ball. Roll on a floured surface. Spread with the margarine. Sprinkle with a mixture of 1/4 cup sugar and cinnamon. Roll as for a jelly roll. Cut into 12 slices. Place cut side down in the prepared pan. Bake at 375 degrees for 20 to 25 minutes or until golden brown.

Yield: 12 servings.

Molasses Bran Muffins with Raisins

1 cup flour
1 teaspoon baking soda
2 cups 100% bran
1 egg, beaten
1 1/4 cups skim milk
1/2 cup dark molasses
1 cup raisins

Combine the flour, baking soda and bran in a bowl; mix well. Stir in a mixture of the egg, skim milk and molasses. Add the raisins; mix well. Spoon evenly into 18 nonstick muffin cups. Bake at 375 degrees for 30 minutes. May add 1 teaspoon salt to the batter.

Yield: 18 servings.

Raspberry Whole Wheat Tea Muffins

1 cup packed light brown sugar
½ cup vegetable oil 1 egg
2 teaspoons vanilla extract
1 cup buttermilk
1½ cups frozen raspberries, chopped
1 cup all-purpose flour
1½ cups whole wheat flour
1 teaspoon baking powder
1 teaspoon baking soda
½ cup chopped pecans
½ cup packed dark brown sugar
¼ cup flour
1 teaspoon cinnamon
2 tablespoons melted butter or margarine

Combine the light brown sugar, oil, egg and vanilla in a large mixer bowl; beat until blended. Stir in the buttermilk and raspberries. Combine the next 4 ingredients in a bowl; add all at once to the raspberry mixture. Stir until blended. Fill greased muffin cups ⅔ full. Combine the remaining ingredients in a bowl; mix well. Sprinkle over the muffins. Bake at 400 degrees for 20 minutes.

Yield: 24 servings.

Sour Cream Muffins

2 cups self-rising flour
½ cup melted margarine
1 cup sour cream

Combine the flour, margarine and sour cream in a medium bowl and mix until thickened and creamy. Spoon evenly into 12 regular or 24 miniature muffin cups. Bake at 400 degrees for 15 to 20 minutes for regular muffins and 12 to 14 minutes for miniature muffins.

Yield: 12 servings.

Miniature Hot Cross Buns

1 (1-pound) loaf frozen bread dough, thawed

2 tablespoons sugar

1/3 cup raisins

3/4 teaspoon cinnamon

1/4 teaspoon nutmeg

1 egg, lightly beaten

1 cup confectioners' sugar

1 tablespoon milk

Knead the bread dough with the sugar, raisins, cinnamon and nutmeg on a lightly floured surface for 10 minutes. Shape into a ball; cover with a damp towel. Let rise for 30 minutes. Shape into 12 rolls. Place on a greased baking sheet. Cover with a damp towel. Let rise for 30 minutes. Brush the buns with the egg. Bake at 375 degrees for 15 minutes or until golden brown. Pipe a mixture of the confectioners' sugar and milk in an X over the top of each bun. Let stand for 30 minutes or until the icing is set.

Yield: 12 servings.

Tortillas de Harina

4 cups flour

2 teaspoons salt

2 teaspoons baking powder

1/4 cup shortening

1 1/2 cups (about) water

Combine the flour, salt and baking powder in a bowl. Cut in the shortening until crumbly. Make a well in the center. Add the water gradually, mixing well. Knead on a floured surface until smooth. Let rest, covered, for 10 minutes. Shape into 12 egg-size balls. Roll each into a 6-inch circle. Heat a griddle or skillet over medium-high heat. Cook tortillas 1 at a time for 1 minute on each side or until lightly speckled.

Yield: 12 servings.

salads
vegetables
sidedishes

Salads • Vegetables • Side Dishes

Mediterranean Artichoke Salad

1 (16-ounce) can artichoke hearts, drained

1/3 cup olive oil

1/3 cup fresh lemon juice

1 head romaine lettuce, torn

4 green onions, chopped

2 tablespoons crushed dried mint

1 cup pitted Greek black olives

1 ripe tomato, peeled, cut into wedges

Salt to taste

Combine the artichoke hearts, olive oil and lemon juice in a shallow bowl. Marinate for 2 to 3 hours in the refrigerator. Combine the lettuce, green onions, mint, olives, tomato and salt in a large salad bowl. Add the artichoke hearts with marinade; toss lightly.

Yield: 6 servings.

Green Beans and Walnuts in Basil Vinaigrette

1 1/2 pounds crisp young green beans, trimmed

Basil Vinaigrette   ***Curly lettuce leaves***

2 green onions, thinly sliced

1/4 cup chopped walnuts

Cook the beans in enough water to cover in a saucepan until tender-crisp. Rinse in ice water and drain. Add Basil Vinaigrette; toss to mix well. Spoon into a serving bowl lined with curly lettuce. Top with green onions and walnuts.

Yield: 6 servings.

Basil Vinaigrette

1 teaspoon pressed garlic

15 basil leaves   ***1/2 teaspoon salt***

1/2 teaspoon freshly ground pepper

1 teaspoon Dijon mustard

1/4 cup each wine vinegar and olive oil

Process the garlic, basil, salt and pepper in a blender for 1 second. Add the mustard and vinegar; process untill well mixed. Add the olive oil in a thin stream, processing until the dressing is thickened.

Yield: 1 cup.

Broccoli and Green Grape Salad

1 bunch broccoli, chopped

1 cup chopped celery

1 cup chopped green onions (optional)

1 cup green grape halves

1/3 cup sugar

1 cup mayonnaise-type salad dressing

1 tablespoon vinegar

Crushed basil leaves to taste

Slivered almonds or pecans

Combine the broccoli, celery, green onions and grapes in a bowl; mix well. Chill, covered, in the refrigerator. Combine the sugar, salad dressing, vinegar and basil in a bowl; mix well. Add to the salad just before serving, tossing to mix. Garnish with nuts.

Yield: 8 servings.

Tropical Cabbage Salad

1 cup flaked coconut

1 medium head cabbage, finely shredded

3/4 cup sour cream

2 1/2 tablespoons vinegar

3/4 teaspoon salt

1/4 teaspoon pepper

1 tablespoon sugar

Paprika to taste

Toasted flaked coconut to taste

Combine 1 cup coconut and cabbage in a salad bowl; mix well. Stir in a mixture of the sour cream, vinegar, salt, pepper and sugar. Sprinkle with the paprika and toasted coconut. May toast coconut by spreading a thin layer of coconut on a baking sheet. Bake at 350 degrees for 3 to 4 minutes or until light brown, stirring frequently.

Yield: 6 servings.

Creamy Caesar Salad

½ (300-gram) package soft tofu

1 clove of garlic, minced

1 teaspoon Worcestershire sauce

1 teaspoon Dijon mustard

2 tablespoons anchovy paste

2 tablespoons lemon juice

3 tablespoons plus 1 teaspoon olive oil

2 tablespoons Parmesan cheese

Salt and pepper to taste

1 head romaine lettuce

1 cup croutons

2 tablespoons Parmesan cheese

Combine the tofu, garlic, Worcestershire sauce, mustard, anchovy paste, lemon juice, olive oil, 2 tablespoons Parmesan cheese, salt and pepper in a blender container. Process until smooth and creamy. Tear the lettuce into bite-size pieces. Place in a salad bowl. Add the prepared dressing and croutons; toss. Sprinkle 2 tablespoons Parmesan cheese over the top.

Yield: 6 servings.

Oriental Turkey Slaw

¼ cup canola oil

2 tablespoons lime juice

2 tablespoons reduced-sodium soy sauce

2 teaspoons sugar

2 teaspoons peanut butter

1 teaspoon minced garlic

¼ to ½ teaspoon red pepper flakes

¾ pound fully-cooked oven-roasted turkey breast, cut into ⅛-inch julienne strips

2 cups packaged coleslaw mix

¼ cup chopped fresh cilantro

¼ cup chopped green onions

Whisk the canola oil, lime juice, soy sauce, sugar, peanut butter, garlic and red pepper flakes in a bowl. Combine the turkey, coleslaw mix, cilantro and onions in a large salad bowl. Add the dressing. Toss gently to mix and serve immediately.

Yield: 8 servings.

Photograph for this recipe is on page 36.

Marinated Tomato Slices

Unpeeled tomatoes, sliced

Sweet onions, sliced

Salt and pepper to taste

Dried basil to taste

1/2 teaspoon sugar

1 teaspoon vinegar

1 teaspoon olive oil

Place a layer of tomatoes in an 8- to 10-inch shallow serving bowl. Top with a layer of onions. Sprinkle with salt, pepper, basil, sugar, vinegar and olive oil. May repeat the layers. Chill for several hours to blend the flavors.

Yield: variable.

Lettuce Stuffed with Cheese and Vegetables

8 ounces cream cheese, softened

1 teaspoon onion juice

Salt and pepper to taste

2 tablespoons Roquefort cheese

2 tablespoons chopped carrot

1 tablespoon chopped green bell pepper

2 tablespoons chopped tomato

1 head lettuce

Blend the cream cheese, onion juice, salt and pepper in a bowl. Mix in the Roquefort cheese, carrot, green pepper and tomato. Cut the lettuce into halves through the core; remove and discard the core. Hollow out the halves, leaving a 1-inch shell. Stuff the lettuce with the cheese mixture. Place the lettuce halves together. Wrap in plastic wrap. Chill in the refrigerator for 8 to 10 hours. Cut into wedges.

Yield: 8 servings.

Layered Garden Pasta Salad

1 (8-ounce) package macaroni shells

1/2 cup sliced green onions

1/4 cup crumbled crisp-cooked bacon

1/4 cup frozen lemon juice

1 cup mayonnaise

1 (2-ounce) envelope dry ranch dressing mix

3 tablespoons grated Parmesan cheese

1 teaspoon sugar

1/2 teaspoon garlic powder

3 cups shredded lettuce 1 cucumber, sliced

1 green bell pepper, chopped

2 medium tomatoes, cut into wedges

Cook the macaroni shells using the package directions. Rinse with cold water; drain well. Combine the macaroni shells, green onions and 2 tablespoons of the bacon in a bowl. Combine the lemon juice, mayonnaise, dressing mix, cheese, sugar and garlic powder in a separate bowl; mix well. Layer the lettuce, macaroni mixture, cucumber and green pepper in a large clear salad bowl. Pour the dressing evenly over the top. Garnish with the tomatoes and the remaining bacon. Chill for 8 to 10 hours in the refrigerator. Dip to the bottom of the bowl to serve.

Yield: 10 servings.

Squash and Pasta Salad

3 cups coarsely chopped yellow summer squash

3 cups rigatoni

2 cups cherry tomato halves

1/2 cup fresh basil leaves

1/4 cup olive oil

2 large cloves of garlic, pressed

3 tablespoons wine vinegar

Salt and pepper to taste

1/4 cup Parmesan cheese

Steam the squash in a vegetable steamer just until tender-crisp. Cool. Cook the rigatoni just until tender using the package directions; rinse with cold water and drain. Mix the squash, rigatoni, tomatoes and basil in a salad bowl. Drizzle a mixture of the olive oil, garlic, vinegar and salt and pepper over the salad. Add the cheese; toss lightly.

Yield: 6 servings.

Zesty Pasta Salad

1 pound pasta, cooked

1 pound feta cheese, crumbled

1 tomato, chopped

1 green bell pepper, chopped

1 (16-ounce) can black olives, drained

1 (16-ounce) bottle zesty Italian salad dressing

1/4 cup grated Parmesan cheese

Combine the pasta, feta cheese, tomato, green pepper and olives in a large bowl; mix well. Add the salad dressing and cheese; mix gently. Chill until serving time.

Yield: 8 servings.

Red Potato Salad with Vegetables

2 pounds unpeeled red potatoes

Salt to taste 1/2 cup chopped onion

1/2 cup chopped celery

1/4 cup chopped green bell pepper

1/2 cup chopped carrot

1/4 cup chopped red bell pepper

1/4 cup chopped dill pickle

1/4 cup sweet pickle relish

1 (2-ounce) jar pimento, drained

1/4 cup plain nonfat yogurt

1/4 cup lite mayonnaise

2 tablespoons Dijon mustard

1/8 teaspoon black pepper

Cayenne pepper to taste

Cook the potatoes in boiling salted water to cover in a saucepan until tender; drain. Chop the potatoes coarsely. Combine the potatoes, onion, celery, green pepper, carrot, red pepper, dill pickle, pickle relish and pimento in a bowl; mix well. Combine the yogurt, mayonnaise, Dijon mustard, black pepper and cayenne pepper in a bowl; mix well. Add to the potato mixture. Toss lightly to mix. Chill, covered, until serving time.

Yield: 10 servings.

Congealed Cinnamon Apple Salad

4 to 6 apples, peeled, sliced

1/2 cup sugar

1 cup water

1/2 cup cinnamon candies

1 (3-ounce) package strawberry gelatin

2 tablespoons mayonnaise

3 ounces cream cheese, softened

1 cup whipped cream

1/2 cup crushed pineapple, drained

1/3 cup finely chopped celery

1/2 cup chopped nuts

Combine the apples, sugar, water and candies in a saucepan. Cook until the apples are tender, stirring frequently. Let stand, covered, for 24 hours in the refrigerator. Drain. Prepare the gelatin using the package directions. Stir in the apple mixture. Pour into a 9x13-inch dish. Chill until firm. Combine the mayonnaise, cream cheese, whipped cream, pineapple, celery and nuts in a bowl; mix well. Spread over the gelatin mixture, sealing to the edges. Chill until serving time. Serve on a lettuce-lined plate.

Yield: 15 servings.

Cranberry Waldorf Salad

1 (3-ounce) package strawberry gelatin

1 cup boiling water

1 cup cranberry sauce

1/2 cup chopped apples

1/2 cup chopped celery

1/4 cup chopped pecans

Mayonnaise

Grated orange peel or chopped pecans

Dissolve the gelatin in the boiling water in a bowl. Add the cranberry sauce, apples, celery and 1/4 cup pecans; mix well. Spoon into a salad mold. Chill until set. Unmold onto a serving plate. Top the servings with a dollop of mayonnaise. Sprinkle with grated orange peel or additional chopped pecans.

Yield: 8 servings.

Molded Spiced Peaches

1 (29-ounce) can sliced peaches
2 to 4 teaspoons vinegar
1 teaspoon whole cloves
2 (2-inch) cinnamon sticks
Water
1 (3-ounce) package orange gelatin
1 cup chopped walnuts
Mayonnaise
Whole walnuts

Combine the undrained peaches, vinegar, cloves, and cinnamon sticks in a saucepan. Bring to a boil over medium heat. Remove from heat. Let stand, covered, for 5 minutes. Remove the peaches. Chill, covered, in the refrigerator. Strain the hot liquid into a glass measure. Add enough water to measure 2 cups. Dissolve the gelatin in the hot liquid. Stir in the chopped walnuts. Arrange 5 or 6 peach slices in each of 6 individual molds. Add the gelatin mixture. Chill until set. Invert onto lettuce-lined salad plates. Garnish with the remaining peaches, a dollop of mayonnaise and whole walnuts. May serve spiced peaches without the gelatin as a meat accompaniment.

Yield: 6 servings.

Avocado Salad with Sweet Vinaigrette Dressing

3 avocados, peeled, sliced
Juice of 1 lemon
3 oranges, peeled, sectioned
2 grapefruit, peeled, sectioned
1 head Bibb lettuce, torn
Sweet Vinaigrette Dressing

Sprinkle the avocado slices with the lemon juice. Arrange the avocados, oranges and grapefruit on lettuce-lined salad plates. Drizzle the dressing over each salad.

Yield: 6 servings.

Sweet Vinaigrette Dressing

1/2 cup vegetable oil
2 tablespoons cider vinegar
2 tablespoons lemon juice
1/2 teaspoon salt
1/4 teaspoon dry mustard
1/4 teaspoon paprika
3 tablespoons confectioners' sugar

Combine all the ingredients in a covered container and shake well. Chill, covered, until serving time.

Layered Overnight Fruit Salad

2 cups shredded lettuce

2 medium Golden Delicious apples, thinly sliced

2 navel oranges

2 cups seedless green grape halves

1/3 cup mayonnaise

1/3 cup sour cream

1 cup shredded Cheddar cheese

Layer the lettuce and apples in a 2-quart serving dish. Peel and section the oranges. Layer the oranges over the apples; squeeze the juice from the orange peel over the oranges. Layer the grapes over the top. Combine the mayonnaise and sour cream in a bowl; mix well. Spread over the fruit; sprinkle with the cheese. Chill, tightly covered with plastic wrap, for 8 to 10 hours. Spoon through the layers to serve.

Yield: 6 servings.

Fruit Salad with Honey and Yogurt Dressing

4 cups coarsely chopped mixed seasonal fruit

1/2 cup toasted unsalted nuts

1/2 cup diced celery

1 cup nonfat plain yogurt

2 tablespoons honey

1/4 teaspoon almond extract

Reserve some of the fruit for garnish. Combine the remaining fruit, nuts and celery in a large bowl. Combine the yogurt, honey and almond extract in a bowl and mix well. Pour over the fruit mixture; toss to coat. Garnish with the reserved fruit.

Yield: 8 servings.

Fresh Fruit Salad

1 apple, sliced

1 small pineapple, cubed

1/2 cantaloupe, cubed

1/2 honeydew melon, cubed

12 strawberries

3 cups watermelon balls or cubes

2 peaches, peeled, sliced

Honey-Lime Dressing

Combine the apple, pineapple, cantaloupe, honeydew melon, strawberries, watermelon and peaches in a large bowl. Chill, covered, in the refrigerator. Pour the Honey-Lime Dressing over the chilled fruit. Serve immediately.

Yield: 8 servings.

Ginger Mayonnaise Dressing

1/2 cup mayonnaise

1/2 cup sour cream

1 teaspoon ground ginger

Combine the mayonnaise, sour cream and ginger in a small bowl; mix well. Chill, covered, until ready to serve.

Yield: 1 cup.

Honey-Lime Dressing

1/2 cup frozen limeade concentrate, thawed

2/3 cup honey

2/3 cup vegetable oil

1 teaspoon poppy seeds

Beat the limeade concentrate, honey, oil and poppy seeds in a small bowl until well mixed. Serve over any favorite combination of fruit salad; toss to coat.

Yield: 2 cups

Garlic-Balsamic Vinaigrette

1 large clove of garlic, minced

1/2 cup extra-light olive oil

1/2 cup vegetable oil

3 tablespoons balsamic vinegar

1/2 teaspoon salt

1/4 teaspoon pepper

Combine the garlic, olive oil, vegetable oil, vinegar, salt and pepper in a jar with a lid. Shake to mix well. Store in the refrigerator.

Yield: 1 1/2 cups.

Mustard Vinaigrette

1/4 cup red wine vinegar

1 1/2 teaspoons vinegar

1 1/2 teaspoons sugar

2 teaspoons dry mustard

1 teaspoon salt

1/4 teaspoon pepper

1/2 teaspoon paprika

1 tablespoon chopped chives

1 tablespoon chopped parsley

1 tablespoon finely chopped onion

1/2 cup vegetable oil

1 ice cube

Combine the wine vinegar, vinegar, sugar, dry mustard, salt, pepper, paprika, chives, parsley, onion, oil and ice cube in a blender container. Process until mixed and slightly thickened.

Yield: 1 cup.

Artichoke Torta

2 (6-ounce) jars marinated artichoke hearts

1 small onion, chopped

1 clove of garlic, chopped

4 eggs, beaten

1/4 cup bread crumbs

1/4 teaspoon salt

1/8 teaspoon pepper

1/8 teaspoon oregano

1/8 teaspoon Tabasco sauce

2 cups shredded sharp Cheddar cheese

2 tablespoons minced parsley

Drain the artichokes, reserving the liquid. Chop the artichokes and sauté with the onion and garlic in the reserved liquid in a skillet for 5 minutes. Combine the remaining ingredients in a bowl; mix well. Layer half the bread crumb mixture, artichokes and remaining bread crumb mixture in a greased 8x12-inch baking dish. Bake at 325 degrees for 30 minutes.

Yield: 8 servings.

Asparagus with Lemon Mayonnaise

1 1/2 pounds fresh asparagus

1/4 cup water

3/4 cup mayonnaise

Juice of 1/2 lemon, or to taste

1 tablespoon capers, rinsed, drained

Rinse the asparagus; break off the tough ends. Arrange the asparagus spears in a 6x10-inch baking dish; add the water. Microwave, tightly covered, on High for 5 to 6 minutes or until tender-crisp, rotating the dish 1/2 turn after 3 minutes. Place the asparagus in cold water in a bowl to cool; drain well. Chill. Combine the mayonnaise, lemon juice and capers in a small bowl. Spoon a small dollop of the sauce on top of each serving of asparagus. Serve with chicken or seafood salad.

Yield: 4 servings.

Green Beans Wrapped in Bacon

1 1/2 pounds fresh green beans

5 slices bacon

3 tablespoons butter, melted

3 tablespoons vinegar

1/2 teaspoon salt

1 teaspoon paprika

1 tablespoon parsley

1 teaspoon finely chopped onion

Snip the ends from the beans; leave whole. Cook in a small amount of boiling water in a saucepan until tender-crisp; drain. Divide into 10 bundles. Cut the bacon into halves. Wrap 1 piece of bacon around each bundle; secure with a wooden pick. Place on a rack in a broiler pan. Broil until the bacon is crisp. Remove to a warm serving platter. Combine the butter and remaining ingredients in a saucepan. Simmer for 1 to 2 minutes. Pour over the hot green bean bundles.

Yield: 10 servings.

Mesquite Baked Beans with Apple and Raisins

2 (16-ounce) cans pork and beans, drained

3/4 cup mesquite barbecue sauce

2 tablespoons golden raisins

1/2 small onion, chopped

1/2 cup packed dark brown sugar

3 bacon slices, chopped

1 tart apple, peeled, chopped

1/2 teaspoon liquid smoke

1/4 teaspoon ginger

Combine the pork and beans, barbecue sauce, raisins, onion, brown sugar, bacon, apple, liquid smoke and ginger in a bowl and mix well. Pour into a 2-quart casserole. Bake, uncovered, at 350 degrees for 1 hour.

Yield: 6 servings.

Spicy Pickled Beets

1/4 cup vinegar
1 onion, chopped
1 teaspoon salt
1 teaspoon sugar
1/4 teaspoon dry mustard
1 teaspoon Worcestershire sauce
1 (16-ounce) can sliced beets, drained

Combine the vinegar, onion, salt, sugar, dry mustard and Worcestershire sauce in a saucepan. Bring to a boil, stirring frequently. Place the beets in a bowl; pour the sauce over the beets. Serve hot or cold.

Yield: 4 servings.

Broccoli Parmigiana

2 eggs, beaten
1 (10-ounce) can cream of mushroom soup
2 (10-ounce) packages frozen chopped broccoli, thawed
1/2 cup milk
1 cup mayonnaise
1 onion, sliced
1 cup Parmesan cheese
1/4 cup margarine
1 1/2 cups herb-seasoned stuffing mix

Combine the eggs, soup, broccoli, milk, mayonnaise and onion in a bowl; mix well. Spoon into a lightly greased 9x14-inch baking dish. Sprinkle the cheese over the top. Melt the margarine in a small skillet. Stir in the stuffing mix. Sprinkle over the cheese layer. Bake at 350 degrees for 35 to 40 minutes or until the topping is golden brown.

Yield: 10 servings.

BROCCOLI-CHEESE SQUARES

8 ounces sharp Cheddar cheese, shredded

8 ounces Monterey Jack cheese, shredded

1/2 cup flour

1 teaspoon baking powder

1/2 teaspoon salt

2 cups small curd cottage cheese

10 eggs, beaten

1 (10-ounce) package frozen chopped broccoli, thawed, drained

3 tablespoons melted butter or margarine

4 egg yolks   4 teaspoons lemon juice

2/3 cup melted butter or margarine

1 tablespoon hot water

Combine the first 5 ingredients in a bowl, tossing to coat the cheese. Mash the cottage cheese in a bowl with a fork. Stir in the cheese mixture, eggs, broccoli and 3 tablespoons butter. Spoon into a buttered 9x13-inch baking dish. Bake at 350 degrees for 40 minutes or until a knife inserted near the center comes out clean. Cool for 10 minutes; cut into squares. Process the egg yolks and lemon juice in a blender until smooth. Add 2/3 cup butter slowly while blender is running. Process until thickened. Add the hot water, processing until smooth. Spoon over the squares.

Yield: 12 servings.

RED CABBAGE WITH APPLES AND RED CURRANT JELLY

1/4 cup unsalted butter

11/2 tablespoons dark brown sugar

2 medium onions, finely chopped

2 small apples, peeled, coarsely chopped

2 medium heads red cabbage, shredded

6 tablespoons red wine vinegar

1 teaspoon coarse salt

11/2 cups meat stock or water

3 tablespoons red currant jelly

Melt the butter in a large heavy skillet over medium heat. Stir in the brown sugar until melted. Add the onions and apples. Cook, covered, over low heat for 5 minutes, stirring twice. Add the cabbage; toss to coat. Add the vinegar, mixing well. Cook, covered, for 10 minutes. Add the salt and 1 cup of the stock. Simmer, covered, over low heat for 11/2 hours or until the cabbage is tender. Add additional stock if necessary to keep moist but not soupy. Add the jelly, stirring until melted. Serve hot. May be stored for up to 2 days in the refrigerator and reheated.

Yield: 8 servings.

Carrots with Gingered Orange Sauce

10 medium carrots, cut into 1-inch diagonal slices

2 tablespoons dark brown sugar

1 tablespoon cornstarch

1/2 teaspoon ground ginger

1/4 teaspoon salt

1 cup orange juice

1/4 cup butter or margarine

Cook the carrots in boiling salted water in a saucepan until tender-crisp; drain. Combine the brown sugar, cornstarch, ginger, salt and orange juice in a small saucepan. Bring to a boil. Cook for 1 minute or until thickened, stirring constantly. Stir in the butter. Pour over the hot carrots, tossing gently to coat.

Yield: 8 servings.

Caribbean Carrots and Sweet Potatoes

2 cups 1/2-inch-thick carrot slices

2 cups cubed peeled sweet potatoes

1 (20-ounce) can juice-pack pineapple chunks

1/4 cup water

2 tablespoons dark brown sugar

1 tablespoon cornstarch

2 teaspoons low-sodium soy sauce

1 teaspoon vinegar

1/2 teaspoon grated orange peel

1/8 teaspoon salt

1/4 cup golden raisins

Steam the carrots in a covered vegetable steamer for 2 minutes. Add the sweet potatoes. Steam, covered, for 8 minutes or until tender-crisp. Drain the pineapple, reserving 1/2 cup juice. Combine the juice, water, brown sugar, cornstarch, soy sauce, vinegar, orange peel and salt in a saucepan. Bring to a boil over medium heat, stirring constantly. Add the pineapple and raisins. Cook for 2 minutes. Combine the steamed vegetables with the pineapple mixture in a large serving bowl and mix gently.

Yield: 6 servings.

Baked Celery and Mushrooms

4 cups diagonally sliced celery

1 (8-ounce) can sliced water chestnuts, drained

4 ounces fresh mushrooms, sliced

1/4 cup slivered almonds

5 tablespoons margarine

3 tablespoons flour

1 cup chicken broth

Salt and pepper to taste

1/2 cup half-and-half

1/2 cup dry bread crumbs

1/2 cup Parmesan cheese

Cook the celery in a small amount of boiling water in a saucepan for 7 minutes or until tender-crisp; drain. Sauté the water chestnuts, mushrooms and almonds in the butter in a large skillet. Stir the flour into the chicken broth. Add to the sautéed mixture. Cook over medium heat until thickened, stirring constantly. Add the salt and pepper. Stir in the celery and half-and-half. Pour into a greased 1 1/2-quart casserole. Sprinkle a mixture of bread crumbs and cheese over the top. Bake at 350 degrees for 30 minutes.

Yield: 8 servings.

Cheese Corn with Southwestern Flavor

1 cup finely chopped onion

1/4 cup margarine

2 (16-ounce) cans whole kernel corn, drained

8 ounces cream cheese, cubed

2 tablespoons salsa

1 (2-ounce) can sliced black olives

8 ounces jalapeño Cheddar cheese, shredded

Sauté the onion in the margarine in a large skillet. Add the corn and cream cheese. Cook over medium heat until the cream cheese is melted, stirring frequently. Add the salsa, olives and cheese. Heat to serving temperature.

Yield: 6 servings.

Sour Cream Baked Corn

2 (8-ounce) packages corn bread muffin mix

1 (17-ounce) can cream-style corn

1 (16-ounce) can whole kernel corn, drained

4 eggs, beaten

1 cup melted margarine

2 cups sour cream

Combine the muffin mix, cream-style corn, whole kernel corn, eggs, margarine and sour cream in a large bowl; mix well. Spoon into a greased 9x13-inch baking dish. Bake at 325 degrees for 1 hour or until a knife inserted near the center comes out clean.

Yield: 12 servings.

Golden Brown Corn Fritters

1 1/3 cups flour

1 1/2 teaspoons baking powder

3/4 teaspoon salt

1 tablespoon sugar

2/3 cup milk

1 egg, beaten

1 (16-ounce) can corn, drained

Vegetable oil for deep-frying

Sift the flour, baking powder, salt and sugar together into a bowl. Add the milk and egg; mix well. Stir in the corn. Drop the batter by tablespoonfuls into the hot oil. Deep-fry for 5 to 8 minutes or until golden brown; drain.

Yield: 12 servings.

Mushrooms Florentine

2 (10-ounce) packages frozen chopped spinach

1/4 cup chopped onion

1/4 cup melted butter or margarine

1 teaspoon salt

1 cup shredded Cheddar cheese

1 pound fresh mushrooms, sliced

2 tablespoons butter or margarine

Garlic powder to taste

Cook the chopped spinach using the package directions. Drain, pressing out the water. Place in a greased 8x11-inch casserole. Sprinkle with the onion, melted butter and salt. Layer 1/2 cup cheese over the spinach. Sauté the mushrooms in 2 tablespoons butter in a skillet. Layer the mushrooms over the spinach. Sprinkle with the garlic powder and remaining cheese. Bake at 350 degrees for 20 minutes.

Yield: 8 servings.

Spicy Okra Skillet Medley

1/2 cup chopped green bell pepper

1/2 cup chopped onion

1 clove of garlic, minced

1 teaspoon vegetable oil

2 cups sliced fresh okra

2 medium tomatoes, seeded, chopped

1 cup fresh corn

2 tablespoons water

1/2 teaspoon chili powder

1/4 teaspoon salt

1/8 teaspoon pepper

Coat a large skillet with nonstick cooking spray. Sauté the green pepper, onion and garlic in hot oil in the prepared skillet over medium heat until the vegetables are tender. Add the okra, tomatoes, corn, water, chili powder, salt and pepper; mix well. Simmer, covered, for 15 minutes or until the corn is tender, stirring occasionally.

Yield: 8 servings.

Baked Parmesan Onions

4 large Vidalia onions

1/4 cup butter, softened

1 teaspoon salt

1/8 teaspoon pepper

Parmesan cheese to taste

Trim and peel each onion. Cut as if to quarter, cutting to but not through the bottom. Press 1 tablespoon butter into center of each onion. Sprinkle with the salt and pepper. Coat with a generous amount of Parmesan cheese. Wrap each onion in foil. Bake at 375 degrees for 1 hour. Serve with roast beef or steak.

Yield: 4 servings.

Green Peas and Cabbage

1 (10-ounce) package frozen green peas

1 teaspoon beef bouillon granules

2 tablespoons hot water

2 cups shredded cabbage

2 tablespoons butter or margarine

1/8 teaspoon dillweed

Salt to taste

Place the peas in a 1 1/2-quart microwave-safe casserole. Mix the bouillon and hot water in a small bowl; pour over the peas. Arrange the cabbage over the peas. Dot with the butter. Cover loosely with plastic wrap. Microwave on High for 8 minutes or until the peas are tender. Stir in the dillweed and salt. Let stand, covered, for 2 minutes before serving.

Yield: 4 servings.

Orange-Glazed Pea Pods

8 ounces fresh pea pods

2 teaspoons sugar

3/4 teaspoon cornstarch

Dash of salt

1/4 cup orange juice

1/2 teaspoon grated orange peel

2 teaspoons butter or margarine

1/2 cup sliced almonds, toasted

Cook the pea pods in a small amount of water in a saucepan until tender-crisp; drain. Combine the sugar, cornstarch and salt in a double boiler. Add the orange juice, blending until smooth. Add the orange peel. Cook until the mixture begins to thicken, stirring constantly. Stir in the butter until melted. Spoon over the pea pods in a serving dish; sprinkle with the almonds.

Yield: 4 servings.

Bell Pepper Casserole

1 cup chopped green bell pepper

1 cup chopped red bell pepper

1 cup chopped onion

1/2 cup milk

3 to 4 drops of Tabasco sauce

1/2 cup seasoned bread crumbs

1 cup shredded sharp Cheddar cheese

Combine the green pepper, red pepper, onion, milk, Tabasco sauce, bread crumbs and cheese in a bowl and mix well. Pour into a greased baking dish. Bake at 350 degrees for 30 minutes.

Yield: 6 servings.

Banana Pepper Bake

3 banana peppers

6 eggs, beaten

1 (16-ounce) can cream-style corn

8 ounces Velveeta cheese, shredded

Slice the peppers. Line a buttered 8x8-inch baking dish with the peppers. Combine the eggs, corn and cheese in a bowl; mix well. Pour over the peppers. Bake at 300 degrees for 45 minutes or until set.

Yield: 8 servings.

Potato Croquettes

4 pounds potatoes

1 cup bread crumbs

2 tablespoons grated Parmesan cheese

5 eggs, beaten

Parsley to taste

1/8 teaspoon salt

1/8 teaspoon pepper

1 cup bread crumbs

Vegetable oil for frying

Cook the potatoes in water to cover in a saucepan until tender. Drain, peel and mash the potatoes. Add 1 cup bread crumbs, cheese, eggs, parsley, salt and pepper; mix well. Shape into croquettes; roll in 1 cup bread crumbs. Fry in hot oil in a deep fryer until golden brown; drain.

Yield: 12 servings.

Microwave Layered Potatoes

8 to 10 medium potatoes, peeled

Chopped green bell pepper to taste

1 or 2 onions, sliced

Garlic salt to taste

1/2 cup margarine

Sour cream

Cut the potatoes lengthwise into slices. Alternate layers of the potatoes, green pepper, onions, garlic salt and dots of margarine in a microwave-safe dish. Microwave on High for 15 minutes, turning several times. Serve with sour cream.

Yield: 4 servings.

Parmesan Potato Wedges

4 large potatoes

1/2 cup bread crumbs

1/2 cup Parmesan cheese

1/2 teaspoon garlic or onion powder

1/2 cup melted margarine

Peel the potatoes; cut lengthwise into wedges. Mix the bread crumbs, cheese and garlic powder in a bowl. Dip the potato wedges into the margarine; coat with the bread crumb mixture. Place potato wedges 1/2 inch apart in a greased 9x13-inch baking dish. Bake at 350 degrees for 45 minutes or until tender and golden brown.

Yield: 4 servings.

Baked Sweet Potatoes with Peach Preserves

6 medium sweet potatoes

1/2 cup peach preserves

1/4 cup butter, softened

1 teaspoon salt

Orange juice

Nutmeg to taste

Place the sweet potatoes in a small greased baking pan. Bake at 350 degrees for 1 hour or until tender. Slice off the top of each potato lengthwise. Scoop out the pulp, leaving the shells intact. Reserve the shells. Place the pulp in a large mixer bowl. Add the preserves, butter and salt; beat until smooth. Add enough orange juice to moisten; mix well. Stuff the reserved shells with the sweet potato mixture. Sprinkle with the nutmeg. Bake at 350 degrees for 20 minutes or until heated through.

Yield: 6 servings.

Sweet Potatoes Chantilly

1 (17-ounce) can sweet potatoes, drained

1 to 2 tablespoons melted butter

Salt and pepper to taste

1/4 to 3/4 cup milk, scalded

1 1/2 cups whipped cream

1/4 cup packed brown sugar

Mash the sweet potatoes in a bowl. Add the butter; mix well. Season with the salt and pepper. Add the milk gradually, beating until smooth and fluffy. Spoon into a greased baking dish. Spread the whipped cream over the potatoes. Sift the brown sugar over the whipped cream. Bake at 375 degrees for 20 to 25 minutes or until bubbly.

Yield: 6 servings.

Ratatouille Niçoise

Olive oil

2 onions, thinly sliced

2 green bell peppers, cut into thin strips

4 cloves of garlic, minced

1 (16-ounce) eggplant, peeled, chopped

2 (8-ounce) zucchini, peeled, chopped

2 pounds tomatoes, peeled, seeded, chopped

Bouquet garni   Salt and pepper to taste

4 sprigs of parsley

Add enough olive oil to a saucepan to cover bottom. Add the onions and green peppers. Sauté until tender but not brown. Add the garlic, eggplant and zucchini. Cook, covered, over medium heat for 15 minutes, stirring occasionally. Add the tomatoes. Tie bouquet garni in a 4-inch square of cheesecloth. Add to the ratatouille with the salt and pepper. Simmer, uncovered, for 35 minutes or until the vegetables are tender and the liquid is thickened, stirring occasionally. Drain the sauce into a saucepan if not thickened to desired consistency, discarding bouquet garni. Simmer until the sauce is thickened, adding tomato paste if desired; adjust seasonings. Stir into vegetable mixture; spoon into a baking dish. Bake at 350 degrees for 15 minutes or until bubbly. Sprinkle with the parsley.

Yield: 10 servings.

Cheesy Summer Squash Casserole

8 ounces summer squash, sliced

Salt to taste

1 large onion, sliced

1/2 teaspoon salt

1/8 teaspoon pepper

2 tablespoons melted margarine

8 ounces sharp Cheddar cheese, coarsely chopped

Combine the squash and salt to taste with a small amount of water in a saucepan. Cook until the squash is tender-crisp; drain. Layer the squash, onion, 1/2 teaspoon salt, pepper, margarine and cheese alternately in a buttered 1-quart baking dish, ending with the cheese. Bake at 400 degrees for 15 to 20 minutes or until light brown and bubbly.

Yield: 4 servings.

Squash Corn Bread Dressing

3 (6-ounce) packages corn bread mix

8 to 10 yellow squash, sliced

1 large onion, chopped

1/4 cup butter or margarine

1 (10-ounce) can cream of celery soup

1 (10-ounce) can cream of mushroom soup

1 (10-ounce) can cream of chicken soup

Pepper to taste

1/2 cup shredded Cheddar cheese

Bake the corn bread using the package directions; cool. Cook the squash and onion in a small amount of boiling water in a large covered saucepan for 15 minutes or until tender; drain. Stir in the butter. Break the corn bread into small pieces in a large bowl. Add the squash and soups; mix well. Add the pepper. Spoon into a greased 9x13-inch baking dish. Sprinkle the cheese over the top. Bake at 350 degrees for 30 minutes.

Yield: 8 servings.

Crustless Garden-Fresh Quiche with Cheese

1 small eggplant, peeled, cut into cubes

1 cup chopped onion

1 large clove of garlic, minced

3 tablespoons vegetable oil

1 small zucchini, sliced

1 teaspoon oregano

1/2 teaspoon salt

1/8 teaspoon pepper

3 tomatoes, chopped 3 eggs, beaten

1 cup shredded mozzarella cheese

1/4 cup grated Parmesan cheese

Sauté the eggplant, onion and garlic in the oil in a large heavy skillet for 10 minutes or until tender. Stir in the zucchini, oregano, salt, pepper and tomatoes. Cook over medium heat for 20 minutes or until the liquid has evaporated, stirring frequently. Cool slightly. Stir the eggs and half the mozzarella cheese into the vegetable mixture. Spoon into a buttered 9-inch pie plate or quiche pan. Top with the remaining mozzarella cheese and Parmesan cheese. Bake at 375 degrees for 25 minutes or until golden brown. Let stand for 10 minutes. Cut into wedges.

Yield: 8 servings.

Three-Cheese Tomato Tart

1/2 cup packed fresh basil
1/2 cup plus 2 tablespoons ricotta cheese
2 eggs, beaten
4 ounces mozzarella cheese, cubed
1/2 cup grated Parmesan cheese
Salt and pepper to taste
2 or 3 tomatoes, sliced
1 partially baked 9-inch pie shell

Process the basil and ricotta cheese in a food processor until the basil is puréed. Add the eggs, mozzarella cheese, Parmesan cheese, salt and pepper. Process until well mixed. Reserve several tomato slices. Layer the remaining tomato slices in a pie shell. Pour the cheese mixture over the tomatoes. Garnish the top with the reserved tomato slices. Bake at 350 degrees for 40 to 50 minutes or until pie shell is brown.

Yield: 6 servings.

Autumn Fruit Salsa

1 cup chopped apple
1 cup chopped pear
1 cup chopped plums
1/2 cup thinly sliced green onions
1 tablespoon lemon juice
1 tablespoon cider vinegar
3 tablespoons unsweetened apple juice
1/2 teaspoon ground ginger
1/4 teaspoon ground coriander
1/4 teaspoon allspice
Crushed red pepper to taste

Combine the apple, pear, plums, green onions and lemon juice in a bowl; mix gently. Add the vinegar, apple juice, ginger, coriander, allspice and red pepper; toss lightly. Let stand at room temperature for 1 hour or longer.

Yield: 6 servings.

Mushroom Walnut Dressing

3 (8-ounce) packages corn bread muffin mix
10 slices white bread, torn into bite-size pieces
1 cup diced onion
2 (8-ounce) cans sliced mushrooms
4 large ribs celery with tops, finely chopped
2 cups chopped English walnuts
Salt and pepper to taste
Sage to taste
Turkey or chicken broth

Bake the muffin mix using the package directions; let cool. Crumble into a large bowl. Add the white bread; mix well. Add the next 4 ingredients and seasonings. Add enough broth to make the mixture moist. Pour into a greased 10x15-inch baking dish. Bake at 350 degrees for 45 to 50 minutes or until brown.

Yield: 16 servings.

West Texas-Style Cheese Grits

2 cups hot cooked grits
2 cups shredded sharp Cheddar cheese
1/2 cup butter
2 cloves of garlic, minced
2 eggs, beaten
1 (4-ounce) can green chiles, minced

Combine the grits, cheese, butter, garlic, eggs and green chiles in a bowl; mix well. Spoon into a greased baking dish. Bake at 300 degrees for 1 hour.

Yield: 8 servings.

Red-Eye Rice

1 cup instant rice
2/3 cup water
1 cup picante sauce
1 (16-ounce) can Mexicorn
1 cup shredded Cheddar cheese
1 cup shredded Monterey Jack cheese
1/2 cup sour cream

Combine the rice, water, picante sauce, Mexicorn, Cheddar cheese, Monterey Jack cheese and sour cream in a bowl and mix well. Pour into a greased 2-quart baking dish. Bake at 350 degrees for 30 minutes.

Yield: 6 servings.

Stir-Fry Chinese Rice

1/2 cup finely chopped cooked ham
2 tablespoons vegetable oil
1 (4-ounce) can mushrooms
4 cups cooked rice
1 green onion, chopped
2 tablespoons soy sauce   1 egg, beaten

Stir-fry the ham in hot oil in a wok. Add the mushrooms, rice, green onion and soy sauce. Stir-fry for 10 minutes. Add the egg. Stir-fry for 5 minutes or until dry and fluffy. May add more soy sauce to taste.

Yield: 8 servings.

Deluxe Rice Amandine

1/2 cup slivered blanched almonds
2 tablespoons butter   2 2/3 cups water
1/2 cup dried cranberries
1 teaspoon salt
2 2/3 cups quick-cooking rice

Sauté the almonds in the butter in a large skillet until golden brown. Add the water, dried cranberries and salt. Bring to a boil. Stir in the rice; remove from the heat. Let stand, covered, for 5 minutes. Fluff with a fork before serving.

Yield: 8 servings.

Skillet Vegetable Pilaf

1/2 cup chopped green bell pepper
1 cup sliced carrots
1/2 cup chopped celery
1 cup chopped tomatoes
1 cup chopped onion
1/3 cup bacon drippings
1 pound sliced bacon, crisp-cooked, crumbled
1/2 teaspoon salt
1/2 teaspoon pepper
1 teaspoon garlic powder
2 cups cooked rice
1/2 cup soy sauce

Sauté the green pepper, carrots, celery, tomatoes and onion in the bacon drippings in a skillet until tender. Add the bacon, salt, pepper, garlic powder and rice; mix well. Stir in the soy sauce. Cook until heated through, stirring constantly.

Yield: 8 servings.

Calabacitas

2 teaspoons chili powder
2 teaspoons cumin
2 or 3 cloves of garlic, minced
Freshly ground pepper to taste
2 tablespoons butter
2 large zucchini, chopped
1 large onion, chopped
1 large tomato, chopped
1 (4-ounce) can chopped green chiles
3/4 cup shredded Monterey Jack cheese

Combine the chili powder, cumin, garlic, pepper and butter in a skillet. Cook over low heat until the butter is melted, stirring constantly. Add the zucchini, onion, tomato and green chiles. Cook until the onion is clear, stirring frequently. Stir in the cheese until melted. Pour into a serving dish.

Yield: 6 servings.

maindishes

Main Dishes

Border Brisket with Vegetables

2 beef briskets

2 (12-ounce) jars chili sauce

Worcestershire sauce to taste

2 packages onion soup mix

3 to 4 pounds potatoes, peeled, coarsely chopped

1 pound carrots, coarsely chopped

2 cans cranberry sauce

Sear the brisket on each side in a skillet over medium heat for 15 minutes or until crispy brown; drain. Line a roasting pan with foil, overlapping the edges. Combine the chili sauce, Worcestershire sauce and onion soup mix in a large bowl, mixing well. Spoon half the mixture into the prepared pan. Place the brisket on the mixture; top with the remaining mixture. Surround with the vegetables. Cover tightly with the foil. Bake at 325 degrees for 2 hours. Uncover; add the cranberry sauce, stirring to make gravy. Bake, covered, for 1½ hours longer. Let stand at room temperature for 15 minutes before slicing. Place on a serving platter; surround with potatoes and carrots. Spoon the gravy over the brisket. Serve the remaining gravy on the side.

Yield: 10 servings.

Broiled Fillet of Beef with Feta and Herb Medallions

½ cup crumbled feta cheese

2 tablespoons softened butter or margarine

1 tablespoon chopped fresh marjoram

1 tablespoon chopped fresh thyme

½ teaspoon Dijon mustard

½ teaspoon lemon juice

Freshly ground lemon pepper to taste

4 (2-inch-thick) beef tenderloin steaks

1 tablespoon olive oil

Salt to taste

Fresh marjoram sprigs

Fresh thyme sprigs

Lemon slices

Combine the first 7 ingredients in a bowl; mix well. Shape into a 3x3-inch log. Wrap in plastic wrap. Chill for 2 to 10 hours. Brush each steak with the olive oil. Sprinkle with salt and lemon pepper. Broil the steaks 5 inches from the heat source for 6 to 8 minutes per side or until medium-rare. Cut the feta cheese mixture into 4 slices. Place 1 slice on top of each steak. Return the steaks to the broiler until the feta cheese mixture is warm and softened. Garnish with the marjoram sprigs, thyme sprigs and lemon slices.

Yield: 4 servings.

Broiled Sirloin with Lemon Butter

1/4 cup butter, softened

1 clove of garlic, minced

1 egg yolk

2 teaspoons minced parsley

1 teaspoon minced onion

1/8 teaspoon thyme

1/8 teaspoon tarragon

2 teaspoons lemon juice

1 teaspoon Dijon mustard

2 (8-ounce) sirloin steaks

Beat the butter, garlic, egg yolk, parsley, onion, thyme and tarragon in a small bowl. Whisk in the lemon juice and mustard. Trim the fat from the steaks, reserving a small amount. Rub the reserved fat over the bottom and side of a hot skillet. Brown the steaks quickly on both sides. Place on a cutting board and cut lengthwise into 1/3-inch slices. Arrange the slices in individual gratin dishes, overlapping slightly. Spread with lemon butter. Broil for 3 minutes or until brown.

Yield: 4 servings.

Lemon Pepper Beef Tenderloin

1 beef tenderloin

Mayonnaise

Garlic salt and lemon pepper to taste

Coat the cold tenderloin with the mayonnaise; sprinkle generously with the garlic salt and lemon pepper. Place on a baking sheet; do not cover. Bake at 500 degrees for 15 minutes for rare, 20 minutes for medium-rare, 25 minutes for medium or 30 minutes for well-done. Turn off the oven. Let the tenderloin stand in the closed oven for 1 hour; do not open oven door.

Yield: 6 servings.

Slow-Cooker Sirloin Cubes with Vegetables

2½ pounds sirloin, cubed

2 large carrots, peeled, sliced

2 medium onions, sliced

1 clove of garlic, minced

1 teaspoon salt

¼ teaspoon pepper

2 bay leaves

1 tablespoon chopped parsley

½ teaspoon thyme

3 (10-ounce) cans condensed beef broth

1 tablespoon tomato paste

8 ounces fresh mushrooms, sliced

2 to 4 tablespoons flour

¾ cup cold water

Combine the sirloin, carrots, onions, garlic, salt, pepper, bay leaves, parsley, thyme, beef broth and tomato paste in a slow cooker. Cook on Low for 7 hours. Add the mushrooms. Cook for 1 hour longer. Remove the bay leaves. Blend the flour with the water. Stir into the sirloin mixture. Cook until thickened, stirring frequently. Serve with wild rice and French bread.

Yield: 6 servings.

Beef and Pork Loaf

½ teaspoon each cumin and nutmeg

2 bay leaves   1 tablespoon salt

1 teaspoon each cayenne and black pepper

½ teaspoon white pepper

¼ cup butter or margarine

2 teaspoons minced garlic

¾ cup minced onion   ½ cup minced celery

½ cup minced green bell pepper

¼ cup minced green onions

1 tablespoon each Tabasco sauce and Worcestershire sauce

½ cup each evaporated milk and catsup

1½ pounds ground beef

8 ounces ground pork   2 eggs, beaten

1 cup fine dry bread crumbs

Mix first 7 seasonings together. Melt the butter in a skillet. Add the seasoning mixture, garlic, minced vegetables, Tabasco sauce and Worcestershire sauce. Sauté for 6 minutes; the mixture will stick. Stir in the evaporated milk and catsup. Cook for 2 minutes longer, stirring to deglaze the skillet. Cool slightly. Remove the bay leaves. Combine the mixture with the remaining ingredients in a bowl; mix well. Shape into a loaf; place in a greased 9x13-inch baking pan. Bake at 350 degrees for 1 hour or until cooked through.

Yield: 8 servings.

Southwestern Lasagna

1½ pounds ground beef
1½ teaspoons cumin
1 tablespoon chili powder
¼ teaspoon garlic powder
¼ teaspoon red pepper
1 teaspoon salt ***1 teaspoon black pepper***
1 (16-ounce) can tomatoes, chopped
10 to 12 corn tortillas
2 cups small curd cottage cheese, drained
1 cup shredded Monterey Jack cheese with peppers
1 egg ***½ cup shredded Cheddar cheese***
2 cups shredded lettuce
½ cup chopped tomatoes
3 green onions, chopped
¼ cup sliced black olives

Brown the ground beef in a skillet, stirring until crumbly; drain. Stir in the next 7 ingredients. Cook over low heat until heated through. Line a 9x13-inch baking dish with ½ of the tortillas. Spoon the ground beef over the tortillas. Top with remaining tortillas. Pour a mixture of the cottage cheese, Monterey Jack cheese and egg over the tortillas. Bake at 350 degrees for 30 minutes. Sprinkle rows of remaining ingredients diagonally across the center.

Yield: 6 servings.

Penne with Sausage and Eggplant

1 (5-ounce) eggplant
8 ounces sweet Italian sausage
¾ cup chopped tomato
½ cup (or more) Wish Bone olive oil vinaigrette salad dressing
2 tablespoons finely chopped cilantro or parsley
8 ounces hot cooked penne, drained
Freshly ground pepper to taste

Cut the eggplant lengthwise into quarters; cut the quarters into ½-inch-thick slices. Cut the sausage into ½-inch-thick slices. Place the sausage in a 3-quart microwave-safe bowl. Microwave on High for 4 minutes, stirring once. Add the eggplant, tomato and salad dressing. Microwave, uncovered, for 5 minutes or until the eggplant is tender, stirring once. Stir in the cilantro. Combine the eggplant mixture with the pasta in a serving bowl, tossing gently to mix. Sprinkle with pepper.

Yield: 6 servings.

Photograph for this recipe is on page 69.

Italian Scaloppine

1½ pounds veal

Flour

1 clove of garlic, minced

2 tablespoons margarine

2 tablespoons olive oil

1 bunch green onions, chopped

8 ounces fresh mushrooms, sliced

2¾ cups chicken broth

¾ cup tomato juice

1 teaspoon chopped fresh parsley

Dash of nutmeg

16 ounces linguini pasta, cooked, drained

Pound the veal. Dredge in the flour. Brown the veal with the garlic in the butter and olive oil in a large skillet. Remove to a plate. Sauté the green onions and mushrooms for 5 minutes. Return the veal to the skillet. Add the broth, tomato juice, parsley and nutmeg. Bring to a boil. Reduce heat to low. Simmer, covered, for 40 minutes. Cook the linguini using the package directions. Top with the veal.

Yield: 6 servings.

Gingered Pork Tenderloin

1 clove of garlic

1 cup soy sauce

1 cup sugar

2 tablespoons fresh ginger, minced

2 green onions, chopped

2 tablespoons sesame seeds

1 whole pork tenderloin

Combine the first 6 ingredients in a medium bowl; mix well. Pour into a shallow dish; add the pork. Chill, covered, for 24 to 48 hours, turning occasionally. Drain the pork; discard the liquid. Place the pork on a rack in a roasting pan. Bake at 350 degrees for 1 hour. Let cool for 15 minutes; slice.

Yield: variable.

Oriental Grilled Pork Chops

1/2 cup teriyaki sauce
1/4 cup minced green onions with tops
1/4 cup lemon juice
2 tablespoons peanut oil
4 cloves of garlic, minced
2 teaspoons crushed red pepper
4 (3/4-inch) pork chops, trimmed

Mix the teriyaki sauce, green onions, lemon juice, peanut oil, garlic and red pepper in a bowl. Pour over the pork chops in a shallow dish. Chill, covered, for 4 hours or longer, turning occasionally. Drain, reserving the marinade. Preheat a grill. Grill 6 to 8 inches from hot coals for 30 to 45 minutes or until cooked through, turning and basting frequently with the marinade.

Yield: 6 servings.

Pork Loin Roast with Apple Plum Sauce

1 (5-pound) center-cut pork loin roast
Salt and pepper to taste
1 (17-ounce) can whole purple plums
1 (15-ounce) jar applesauce
1/4 teaspoon pumpkin pie spice
1/8 teaspoon cinnamon

Sprinkle the pork with the salt and pepper; place on a rack in a shallow roasting pan. Roast at 325 degrees for 30 to 35 minutes per pound or to 170 degrees on a meat thermometer. Drain the plums, reserving 1/4 cup syrup; discard the pits. Process the plums with the reserved syrup in a blender at medium speed for 1 minute. Combine the plum purée with the applesauce, pumpkin pie spice and cinnamon in a saucepan. Heat to serving temperature. Serve over the pork.

Yield: 12 servings.

Baked Ham with Horseradish Glaze

5½ to 6 pounds fully cooked boneless ham

1 cup packed light brown sugar

Whole cloves to taste

⅓ cup horseradish

¼ cup lemon juice

Have the butcher slice the ham into ¼-inch-thick slices. Reassemble the ham and tie with a cord. Place the ham on a rack in a shallow baking dish. Bake at 325 degrees for 1½ hours. Mix the brown sugar, cloves, horseradish and lemon juice in a small saucepan. Bring to a boil. Pour over the ham. Increase the oven temperature to 400 degrees. Bake for 15 minutes longer, basting occasionally with the glaze.

Yield: 10 servings.

Ham and Cheese Strata

12 slices bread

12 ounces sharp Cheddar cheese, sliced

Florets of ½ bunch broccoli

2 cups chopped cooked ham

6 eggs, lightly beaten

3½ cups milk

1 teaspoon finely chopped onion

¼ teaspoon dry mustard

¼ teaspoon salt

Trim the crusts from the bread. Arrange 6 slices in a greased 9x13-inch baking dish. Layer the cheese, broccoli and ham in the prepared dish; top with the remaining bread. Beat the eggs, milk, onion, dry mustard and salt in a mixer bowl. Pour over the layers. Bake at 325 degrees for 55 minutes.

Yield: 12 servings.

Ham and Six-Cheese Quiche

1 recipe (2-crust) pie pastry

12 eggs, beaten

8 ounces cream cheese, softened

4 cups heavy cream

1 pound ham, finely chopped

2 cups ricotta cheese

3 cups shredded mozzarella cheese

2 cups shredded Cheddar cheese

2 cups shredded Swiss cheese

2 cups shredded American cheese

1/4 to 1/2 cup melted butter

1 medium onion, finely chopped

Salt and pepper to taste

Line a greased 9x13-inch baking dish with the pie pastry. Beat the eggs with the cream cheese and cream in a mixer bowl. Stir in the ham, ricotta cheese, mozzarella cheese, Cheddar cheese, Swiss cheese, American cheese, butter, onion, salt and pepper. Pour into the prepared baking dish. Bake at 350 degrees for 40 minutes or until a knife inserted near the center comes out clean.

Yield: 10 servings.

Tennessee Ham and Apple Bake

3 cups diced cooked ham

4 medium tart apples, sliced

1/4 cup packed dark brown sugar

1/4 teaspoon ground mace

1/4 cup apple juice or water

1 cup pancake mix

1 cup milk

2 tablespoons melted butter or margarine

Layer half the ham and apples in a 2-quart casserole. Combine the brown sugar and mace in a small bowl. Sprinkle half the brown sugar mixture over the apples. Repeat the layers. Pour the apple juice over the casserole. Bake at 350 degrees for 40 minutes or until the apples are tender. Combine the pancake mix, milk and butter in a medium bowl; blend well. Pour over the casserole. Bake, uncovered, for 20 minutes longer or until puffed and golden brown.

Yield: 6 servings.

Indonesian Chicken and Shrimp with Peanut Sauce

2 tablespoons soy sauce
2 tablespoons lime juice
1 tablespoon dark molasses
1 tablespoon curry powder
1 teaspoon dried minced garlic
8 ounces boneless skinless chicken breasts
8 ounces large shrimp, shelled, deveined
1 cup fresh pineapple chunks
1 cup red bell pepper chunks
Peanut Sauce

Combine the soy sauce, lime juice, molasses, curry powder and garlic in a bowl and mix well. Rinse the chicken and pat dry. Pierce the chicken with a fork in several places on both sides. Cut the chicken into 3/4-inch cubes. Add to the soy sauce mixture, stirring to coat. Let stand for 10 minutes. Preheat the broiler. Drain the chicken, reserving the marinade. Thread the chicken, shrimp, pineapple and red pepper alternately onto skewers. Place on a rack in a broiler pan. Broil 4 to 5 inches from the heat for 8 to 10 minutes, turning and basting occasionally with the reserved marinade. Serve with the Peanut Sauce.

Yield: 4 servings.

Peanut Sauce

1 cup chicken broth
1/2 cup creamy peanut butter
1/4 cup sweetened flaked coconut
1/2 teaspoon ground cumin
1/2 teaspoon ground coriander
1/2 teaspoon dried minced garlic
1/8 teaspoon ground red pepper

Combine the chicken broth, peanut butter, coconut, cumin, coriander, garlic and red pepper in a saucepan. Cook over medium heat for 2 to 3 minutes or until thickened, stirring occasionally.

Photograph for this recipe is on page 70.

Chicken with Artichokes and Hearts of Palm

10 boneless skinless chicken breasts
Salt and pepper to taste
1 (4-ounce) can mushroom caps, drained
1 (14-ounce) can artichoke hearts, drained, quartered
1 (7-ounce) jar hearts of palm, cut into thirds
1 (8-ounce) can sliced water chestnuts, drained
1 (10-ounce) can cream of asparagus soup
1/2 cup chicken broth
1 cup sour cream
Paprika to taste

Rinse the chicken and pat dry. Arrange in a greased 9x13-inch baking dish. Season with the salt and pepper. Layer the mushrooms, artichokes, hearts of palm and water chestnuts over the chicken. Combine the soup, broth and sour cream in a small bowl; mix well. Pour the soup mixture over the layers in the baking dish. Sprinkle with the paprika. Bake, covered, at 350 degrees for 30 minutes. Bake, uncovered, for 30 minutes longer or until the chicken is tender. Serve with rice or noodles.

Yield: 10 servings.

Baked Lemon Chicken

1 cup fat-free sour cream
4 1/2 tablespoons lemon juice
1 1/2 teaspoons celery salt
1/4 teaspoon paprika
2 teaspoons Worcestershire sauce
Salt and pepper to taste
8 boneless skinless chicken breasts
3 cups Italian bread crumbs
1/2 cup melted margarine

Combine the sour cream, lemon juice, celery salt, paprika, Worcestershire sauce, salt and pepper in a bowl; mix well. Rinse the chicken and pat dry. Place in a shallow bowl. Pour the sour cream mixture over the chicken. Marinate for 8 to 10 hours in the refrigerator, turning occasionally. Roll each chicken breast in the bread crumbs to coat. Place in a greased 9x13-inch baking dish. Drizzle the margarine over the chicken. Bake at 350 degrees for 1 1/4 hours.

Yield: 8 servings.

Chicken and Herb-Seasoned Dressing

4 whole boneless skinless chicken breasts

2 (10-ounce) cans creamy chicken-mushroom soup

1 (8-ounce) package herb-seasoned stuffing mix

1/2 cup melted butter or margarine

Rinse the chicken. Cook in water to cover in a large saucepan for 1 hour or until tender. Strain the broth, reserving 2 2/3 cups. Chop the chicken into bite-size pieces. Mix the soup with the reserved broth. Combine the stuffing mix with the butter in a bowl; mix well. Reserve 1/4 cup stuffing mixture. Layer the remaining stuffing mixture, chicken and soup mixture 1/2 at a time in a greased 9x13-inch baking dish. Top with the reserved stuffing mixture. Chill, covered, for 8 to 10 hours. Let stand at room temperature for 15 minutes. Bake at 350 degrees for 30 to 45 minutes or until heated through.

Yield: 8 servings.

Chicken Taco and Rice

1 pound chicken breast fillets, cut into strips

2 tablespoons corn oil

1 (13-ounce) can chicken broth

1 (8-ounce) can tomato sauce

1 envelope taco seasoning mix

1 (12-ounce) can corn, drained

1 medium red bell pepper, cut into strips

1 1/2 cups uncooked instant rice

1/2 cup shredded Cheddar cheese

Tortilla chips

Rinse the chicken and pat dry. Sauté the chicken in the corn oil in a skillet for 2 minutes. Add the broth, tomato sauce and taco seasoning mix. Bring to a boil. Simmer, covered, over low heat for 5 minutes, stirring occasionally. Add the corn and red pepper. Bring to a boil. Stir in the rice. Cover; remove from the heat. Let stand for 5 minutes. Fluff with a fork. Pour into a serving bowl. Sprinkle with the cheese. Serve with the tortilla chips.

Yield: 4 servings.

Chicken Tetrazzini

8 ounces uncooked spaghetti, broken
4 boneless skinless chicken breasts, cooked
1 (8-ounce) can mushrooms, drained
1/4 cup chopped onion
1/4 cup chopped celery
1/2 cup margarine
2 (10-ounce) cans cream of chicken soup
2 cups sour cream (optional)
Grated Parmesan cheese
Paprika to taste

Cook the spaghetti using the package directions. Arrange in a buttered baking dish. Chop the chicken into bite-size pieces. Sauté the mushrooms, onion and celery in the margarine in a skillet. Stir in the chicken, soup and sour cream. Spoon over the spaghetti. Top with the cheese and paprika. Bake at 350 degrees for 40 minutes.

Yield: 6 servings.

Curried Chicken in Patty Shells

6 baked patty shells
6 chicken breast fillets
Salt and pepper to taste
Garlic powder to taste
Curry powder to taste
Flour
1/4 cup butter
8 ounces fresh mushrooms, thickly sliced
Grated peel and juice of 1 lemon
1 1/2 cups chicken broth
1 tablespoon cornstarch
Chopped tomato and parsley

Keep the patty shells warm. Rinse the chicken; pat dry. Cut the chicken into 1-inch strips. Sprinkle with the salt, pepper, garlic powder and curry powder. Coat with the flour. Brown the chicken in the butter in a skillet. Do not overcook the chicken. Add the mushrooms, lemon peel and juice. Simmer for 5 minutes. Add a mixture of the chicken broth and cornstarch. Cook until thickened, stirring constantly. Spoon into the warm patty shells. Garnish with the chopped tomato and parsley.

Yield: 6 servings.

Honey Dijon Chicken

6 boneless skinless chicken breasts

1 jar low-fat honey Dijon salad dressing

3 cups assorted vegetables: potatoes, onions, parsnips, turnips, etc.

1/4 cup chopped fresh parsley

2 tablespoons fresh chives

Salt and pepper to taste

Honey

1 lemon, sliced

Rinse the chicken; pat dry. Place in a shallow bowl. Spread the salad dressing over the chicken. Marinate the chicken for 6 to 8 hours. Place the chicken in a greased roasting pan with desired vegetables. Pour remaining salad dressing over all. Add the parsley, chives, salt and pepper. Drizzle the honey over the top. Arrange the lemon slices on top. Squeeze the lemon ends over the honey. Bake at 350 degrees for 1 hour.

Yield: 6 servings.

Grilled Jamaican Chicken

1 tablespoon each allspice and thyme

1 1/2 teaspoons cayenne pepper

1 1/2 teaspoons black pepper

1 1/2 teaspoon sage   3/4 teaspoon nutmeg

3/4 teaspoon cinnamon

2 tablespoons each salt and garlic powder

1 tablespoon sugar   1/4 cup olive oil

1/4 cup soy sauce   3/4 cup white vinegar

1/2 cup orange juice   1/4 cup lime juice

1 Scotch bonnet pepper, seeded. chopped

1 white onion, finely chopped

3 green onions, finely chopped

4 large chicken breasts

Combine the first 10 ingredients in a bowl; mix well. Add the olive oil, soy sauce, vinegar, orange juice and lime juice gradually, blending with a wire whisk. Stir in the Scotch bonnet pepper, onion and green onions. Rinse the chicken and pat dry. Place in a shallow bowl. Add the marinade. Marinate in the refrigerator for 1 hour or longer; drain, reserving the marinade. Grill the chicken on a grill for 6 to 8 minutes on each side, basting with the reserved marinade. Heat the leftover marinade to serve with the chicken.

Yield: 4 servings.

Pecan-Stuffed Chicken Breasts

1 large rib celery, chopped

1 small onion, minced

2 tablespoons butter or margarine

1/2 teaspoon salt

1/4 teaspoon pepper

2 cups dry bread crumbs

1 cup coarsely chopped pecans

2 teaspoons chopped parsley

1/4 cup water

4 whole boneless skinless chicken breasts

2 tablespoons lemon juice

Salt and pepper to taste

Sauté the celery and onion in the butter in a skillet over medium heat until soft. Add 1/2 teaspoon salt and 1/4 teaspoon pepper. Stir in the bread crumbs, pecans, parsley and water. Rinse the chicken and pat dry. Place each piece of chicken on a double foil square; brush both sides with the lemon juice. Sprinkle with salt and pepper to taste. Spoon 1/4 of the stuffing in the center of each piece of chicken; close the foil tightly. Place on a baking sheet. Bake at 400 degrees for 20 minutes. Open the bundles; brush with the drippings. Bake, uncovered, for 20 minutes longer.

Yield: 4 servings.

Sweet-and-Sour Chicken Oriental

1 (4-ounce) jar sweet and sour sauce

1 envelope onion soup mix

1 (16-ounce) can whole cranberry sauce

8 chicken breast fillets

Mix the sweet-and-sour sauce, onion soup mix and cranberry sauce in a bowl. Rinse the chicken and pat dry. Place in a greased baking dish. Pour the sauce over the chicken. Bake, covered, at 350 degrees for 30 minutes. Bake, uncovered, for 30 minutes longer.

Yield: 8 servings.

West Indian Chicken with Chutney

4 boneless skinless chicken breasts

1 teaspoon rum extract

Grated peel and juice of 2 limes

4 tablespoons chutney

1 cup bread crumbs

4 to 6 tablespoons butter

Rinse the chicken and pat dry. Flatten the chicken with a meat mallet. Place in a shallow bowl. Combine the extract, lime peel and juice. Pour over the chicken. Marinate, covered, in the refrigerator for 2 hours or longer. Drain the chicken, reserving the marinade. Spoon 1 tablespoon chutney onto each piece of chicken. Roll and secure with a wooden pick. Dip into the marinade and coat with the bread crumbs. Brown in the butter in a skillet. Arrange in a shallow baking dish. Top with the remaining marinade. Bake at 375 degrees for 30 minutes, basting several times with the pan drippings.

Yield: 4 servings.

Turkey Breast Cutlets with Artichoke Hearts

4 turkey breast cutlets

1 cup Italian bread crumbs

2 to 6 tablespoons margarine

1½ cups chicken broth

1 large onion, sliced into half-rings

1 (16-ounce) can artichoke hearts, drained

Pepper to taste

3 tablespoons chopped fresh parsley

Rinse the cutlets and pat dry. Coat with the bread crumbs. Brown lightly on both sides in 2 tablespoons margarine in a skillet over medium heat, adding additional margarine as needed. Remove to a greased shallow baking dish. Add the chicken broth to the skillet, stirring to deglaze. Add the onion, artichokes and pepper. Cook for 2 minutes or until heated through. Remove the artichokes and onion to top of cutlets; pour cooking liquid over top. Bake, covered, at 300 degrees for 20 minutes. Garnish with the parsley.

Yield: 4 servings.

Indonesian Baked Turkey with Teriyaki Peanut Sauce

1 (2½- to 3-pound) boneless turkey breast
⅓ cup chunky peanut butter
⅓ cup teriyaki sauce
¼ cup lemon juice   ¼ cup vegetable oil
2 teaspoons ground ginger
2 teaspoons basil
2 teaspoons onion powder
2 teaspoons garlic powder
¼ to ½ teaspoon crushed red pepper

Rinse the turkey and pat dry. Place in a sealable plastic bag. Process the peanut butter, teriyaki sauce, lemon juice, oil, ginger, basil, onion powder, garlic powder and red pepper in a blender or food processor until smooth. Reserve ½ cup of the marinade. Pour the remaining marinade over the turkey; seal tightly. Invert the plastic bag to coat. Marinate in the refrigerator for 30 minutes. Drain, reserving the marinade. Place the turkey in a greased baking pan. Bake at 400 degrees for 1 to 1½ hours or until cooked through, basting occasionally with the marinade drained from the turkey. Let stand for 10 minutes before slicing. Heat the ½ cup reserved marinade. Serve with the turkey.

Yield: 8 servings.

Baked Lobster with Shrimp

1 cup mayonnaise
½ teaspoon salt
⅛ teaspoon pepper
1 teaspoon Worcestershire sauce
¼ cup chopped green bell pepper
¼ cup chopped onion
1 cup chopped celery
1 cup coarsely chopped cooked lobster
6 ounces peeled cooked shrimp
1 cup buttered bread crumbs

Combine the mayonnaise, salt, pepper and Worcestershire sauce in a bowl; mix well. Stir in the green pepper, onion, celery, lobster and shrimp. Spoon into greased baking shells or ramekins. Sprinkle with the bread crumbs. Bake at 350 degrees for 30 minutes or until brown.

Yield: 8 servings.

Lobster Sauce with Pasta

16 ounces chunk lobster
1/2 small purple onion, chopped
Lemon pepper to taste
2 tablespoons olive oil
Florets of 1 bunch broccoli
1 red bell pepper, chopped
1 (6-ounce) can mushrooms, drained
3 tablespoons butter
2 tablespoons ranch salad dressing mix
16 ounces pasta, cooked, drained

Stir-fry the lobster, onion and lemon pepper in the olive oil in a skillet. Remove to a platter. Stir-fry the broccoli, red pepper and mushrooms in a skillet. Add the lobster mixture; mix well. Stir in the butter and salad dressing mix. Stir-fry over low heat until heated through. Serve over the pasta.

Yield: 6 servings.

Cajun Rosemary Shrimp

1 cup melted butter
1/4 cup Worcestershire sauce
1/4 cup pepper
1 teaspoon rosemary
1/4 teaspoon hot pepper sauce
2 teaspoons salt
1 clove of garlic, minced
Juice of 1 lemon
1 1/2 pounds unpeeled shrimp
1 lemon, sliced

Mix the butter, Worcestershire sauce, pepper, rosemary, hot pepper sauce, salt, garlic and lemon juice in a bowl. Pour 1/4 cup of the sauce into a large greased baking dish. Arrange the shrimp and lemon slices over the top. Drizzle with the remaining sauce. Bake at 400 degrees for 20 minutes or until the shrimp turn pink, stirring 1 or 2 times.

Yield: 4 servings.

Shrimp Cantonese with Cheese Rice Ring

1 (14-ounce) can pineapple chunks
1/4 cup sugar   2 tablespoons cornstarch
1/4 cup vinegar   2 teaspoons soy sauce
2 ribs celery, chopped
4 green onions, sliced
1/2 green bell pepper, cut into 1/4-inch strips
1 1/2 pounds peeled cooked jumbo shrimp
1 tomato, cut into wedges
1 cup rice, cooked
1 1/2 cups shredded Swiss cheese
1/3 cup toasted sliced almonds

Drain the pineapple, reserving the juice. Add enough water to the reserved juice to measure 1 cup. Combine the juice mixture with the sugar and cornstarch in a saucepan. Stir in the vinegar and soy sauce gradually. Cook over medium heat until thickened, stirring constantly. Stir in the pineapple, celery, green onions, green pepper, shrimp and tomato. Cook until heated through. Combine the hot rice with the cheese in a bowl. Pack into a buttered 4-cup mold. Invert immediately onto a serving plate. Top with the shrimp mixture; sprinkle with almonds.

Yield: 6 servings.

Curried Lemon Shrimp

1/3 cup butter
3 tablespoons flour
2 teaspoons curry powder
1/2 teaspoon salt
1/4 teaspoon paprika
1/8 teaspoon nutmeg
2 cups half-and-half
3 cups peeled cooked shrimp
2 teaspoons freshly grated or finely chopped ginger
1 tablespoon lemon juice
1/8 teaspoon Worcestershire sauce

Melt the butter in a saucepan over low heat. Stir in the flour, curry powder, salt, paprika and nutmeg. Stir in the half-and-half gradually. Cook until thickened, stirring constanty. Stir in the shrimp, ginger, lemon juice and Worcestershire sauce. Serve with baked rice and condiments such as raisins, flaked coconut, ground peanuts and chopped Granny Smith apples.

Yield: 4 servings.

Orange Roughy with Gingered Shrimp Sauce

1/3 cup mayonnaise
1/3 cup sour cream
1/2 teaspoon dried minced onion
1/4 teaspoon ground ginger
1/4 teaspoon dillweed
Dash of salt
1/4 cup peeled boiled small shrimp
1 pound orange roughy
1 tablespoon margarine
1/4 cup toasted sliced almonds
Lemon wedges
Fresh dill sprigs

Mix the mayonnaise, sour cream, onion, ginger, dillweed, salt and shrimp in a microwave-safe dish. Chill, covered, for 1 hour. Brown the roughy in the margarine in a skillet for 5 to 7 minutes or until the fish flakes easily. Keep warm in a serving dish. Microwave the shrimp mixture for 3 minutes, stirring after each minute. Spoon over the roughy. Sprinkle with the almonds. Garnish with the lemon wedges and dill.

Yield: 4 servings.

Baked Salmon Fillets with Lime and Ginger

1 1/4 pounds salmon fillets
3 teaspoons minced fresh gingerroot
2 teaspoons minced lime peel
3 tablespoons fresh lime juice
Freshly ground pepper to taste

Line a large broiler pan or baking sheet with foil; spray lightly with nonstick cooking spray. Rinse the salmon and pat dry. Remove any bones. Slice diagonally into 1/2- to 1-inch-thick pieces. Arrange the salmon in the center of the baking pan with pieces touching. Sprinkle with the gingerroot and lime peel; drizzle with the lime juice. Bake at 500 degrees for 3 to 4 minutes or until the salmon is opaque throughout. Sprinkle with pepper. Serve immediately.

Yield: 4 servings.

Marinated Salmon Steaks on the Grill

1 ounce sun-dried tomatoes
1 cup water
1/2 teaspoon minced garlic
2 tablespoons catsup
2 tablespoons tomato paste
2 tablespoons balsamic vinegar
2 tablespoons cider vinegar
2 tablespoons fresh lemon juice
1/2 cup water
1/4 cup vegetable oil
1 1/2 teaspoons minced fresh parsley
1 1/2 teaspoons minced drained capers
1 tablespoon minced fresh chives
1/2 teaspoon crumbled dried tarragon
1/4 teaspoon salt
1/2 teaspoon freshly ground black pepper
1/8 teaspoon cayenne pepper
4 (8-ounce) salmon steaks, 1 inch thick
1/2 cup water

Simmer the tomatoes in 1 cup water in a saucepan for 3 minutes; cool to room temperature. Drain and chop the tomatoes, reserving the cooking liquid. Combine the reserved liquid, tomatoes, and next 15 ingredients in a bowl; mix well. Chill, covered, for 2 to 12 hours. Place the salmon in a shallow dish. Add 1/2 cup water to the marinade, mixing well. Pour over the salmon, turning the salmon to coat. Marinate in the refrigerator for 2 hours, turning occasionally. Drain, reserving the marinade. Grill the salmon 4 inches from the heat source for 13 minutes or just until cooked through, turning halfway through the cooking time and brushing with the reserved marinade. Heat any remaining marinade in a small saucepan. Serve with the salmon. Do not use oil-pack sun-dried tomatoes in this recipe.

Yield: 4 servings.

Scallops in Lime Watercress Sauce

3/4 cup beef broth

1/2 onion, sliced

1 sprig of parsley

1 bay leaf

Salt and lemon pepper to taste

1 pound sea scallops

Lime Watercress Sauce

Combine the broth, onion, parsley, bay leaf, salt and lemon pepper in a large saucepan. Bring to a boil over medium heat. Add the scallops. Simmer over low heat for 6 minutes or just until cooked through. Do not overcook. Drain the scallops and place in a bowl. Chill, covered, for 1 hour. Mix the scallops with the Lime Watercress Sauce just before serving.

Yield: 6 servings.

Lime Watercress Sauce

4 green onions, chopped

1/2 cup mayonnaise

1/4 cup watercress leaves

2 tablespoons chopped fresh parsley

2 tablespoons chopped fresh chives

1 1/2 teaspoons chopped fresh dill

Juice of 1/2 lime

Combine the green onions, mayonnaise, watercress, parsley, chives, dill and lime juice in a blender container; process until smooth. Chill, covered, for 1 hour or longer.

Scallop and Mushroom Stir-Fry with Pasta

8 ounces scallops

8 ounces fresh mushrooms, sliced

1 small onion, chopped

1/2 cup chopped red or green bell pepper

1 tablespoon butter or margarine

1 tablespoon vegetable oil

1/8 teaspoon nutmeg

1/8 teaspoon salt

1/8 teaspoon pepper

1 cup plain yogurt

1/4 cup grated Parmesan cheese

8 ounces spaghetti

Sauté the scallops, mushrooms, onion and bell pepper in the butter and oil in a skillet for 5 minutes or until the scallops are cooked through and the vegetables are tender. Stir in the nutmeg, salt, pepper, yogurt and cheese. Cook the spaghetti using the package directions. Place in a serving bowl. Top with the hot scallop mixture.

Yield: 4 servings.

Pan-Fried Tuna Cakes with Lemon-Dill Sauce

1 (12-ounce) can water-packed tuna

3/4 cup seasoned bread crumbs

1/4 cup minced green onions

2 tablespoons chopped pimentos

1/4 cup egg substitute 1/2 cup skim milk

2 tablespoons margarine

1/4 cup chicken broth

1 tablespoon lemon juice

1/4 teaspoon crumbled dried dillweed

Lemon slices Fresh parsley sprigs

Drain and finely flake the tuna. Combine the tuna, bread crumbs, green onions and pimentos in a large bowl. Beat the egg substitute and milk together in a small bowl. Stir into the tuna mixture, mixing just until moistened. Shape with lightly floured hands into eight 4-inch patties. Melt the margarine in a large nonstick skillet. Fry the patties a few at a time for 3 minutes on each side or until golden brown. Keep warm in a 300-degree oven until ready to serve. Combine the chicken broth, lemon juice and dillweed in a small saucepan. Cook until heated through. Spoon over the tuna cakes. Garnish with the lemon and parsley.

Yield: 4 servings.

Garlic-Mustard Grilled Tuna

4 (1-inch) tuna steaks

Salt and pepper to taste

Mustard Marinade

4 sprigs of fresh dill for garnish

4 lime slices for garnish

1 cup salsa

Rub both sides of the tuna steaks with the salt and pepper; place in a large glass baking dish. Pour the Mustard Marinade over the steaks. Marinate, covered, in the refrigerator for 2 hours or longer, turning occasionally. Remove the tuna and reserve the marinade. Place the tuna on a rack in a broiler pan or on a grill. Broil or grill 6 inches from the heat source for 4 to 6 minutes on each side or until firm, basting frequently with the reserved marinade. Garnish with the dill sprigs and lime. Serve with the salsa.

Yield: 4 servings.

Mustard Marinade

2 tablespoons Dijon mustard

2 cloves of garlic, minced

1/2 cup olive oil

Juice of 4 limes

1/4 cup soy sauce

1 teaspoon freshly ground pepper

1 tablespoon chopped fresh dill

Combine the mustard, garlic, olive oil, lime juice, soy sauce, pepper and dill in a bowl; mix well.

Garlic Eggplant Scaloppine

2½ cups chopped onions

3 tablespoons olive oil

6 cups chopped eggplant

1 medium green bell pepper, chopped

12 ounces mushrooms, chopped

1 tablespoon dried basil

1 tablespoon vegetable bouillon granules

1 cup boiling water

1 (28-ounce) can whole tomatoes with sauce

5 cloves of garlic, minced

Pepper to taste

16 ounces pasta, cooked, drained

Parmesan cheese

Sauté the onions in the olive oil in a large deep saucepan over medium heat for 5 minutes or until tender. Add the eggplant, green pepper, mushrooms and basil. Cook for 15 minutes or until the eggplant is tender, stirring occasionally. Combine the bouillon granules and boiling water in a bowl, stirring until dissolved. Add the bouillon, tomatoes, garlic and pepper to the eggplant mixture. Simmer for 10 to 15 minutes longer. Serve over the pasta. Garnish with the Parmesan cheese.

Yield: 6 servings.

Mushrooms Florentine

1 pound small fresh mushrooms

¼ cup butter   2 tablespoons lemon juice

2 tablespoons chopped green onions

2 teaspoons chopped dillweed

1 clove of garlic, minced

Salt and pepper to taste

2 tablespoons water

3 ounces cream cheese, softened

1 cup sour cream

1 cup crumbled feta cheese

1 (10-ounce) package frozen chopped spinach

¼ cup butter

4 slices dry bread, coarsely crumbled

Sauté the mushrooms in ¼ cup butter in a skillet over medium heat for 3 minutes. Add the lemon juice, green onions, dillweed, garlic, salt and pepper. Cook for 3 minutes longer. Add the water and cream cheese. Cook over low heat until the cream cheese is melted, stirring constantly. Stir in the sour cream, feta cheese and spinach. Spoon into a greased casserole. Melt ¼ cup butter in a skillet over medium heat. Add the bread crumbs. Stir-fry for 3 to 4 minutes or until golden brown. Sprinkle over the casserole. Bake at 350 degrees for 30 minutes.

Yield: 6 servings.

Mushroom Stroganoff

1 onion, sliced

8 ounces mushrooms, sliced

1 clove of garlic, minced

1 tablespoon vegetable oil

1 tablespoon butter or margarine

2 tablespoons vegetable bouillon granules

1 1/2 cups boiling water

2 tablespoons catsup

1 teaspoon Worcestershire sauce

3 tablespoons flour

1 cup sour cream

4 cups cooked egg noodles

Sauté the onion, mushrooms and garlic in the oil and butter in a skillet for 5 minutes. Stir the bouillon granules into the boiling water until dissolved. Stir 1 cup of the vegetable bouillon, catsup and Worcestershire sauce into the mushroom mixture. Blend the flour with the remaining bouillon; add to the mushroom mixture. Bring to a boil over medium heat. Simmer over low heat for 1 minute, stirring constantly. Add the sour cream. Cook until heated through. Serve over the noodles.

Yield: 4 servings.

Tomato and Squash Quiche

2 cups sliced zucchini

1 cup chopped tomato

1/2 cup chopped onion

1/3 cup Parmesan cheese

1 1/2 cups milk

3/4 cup buttermilk baking mix

3 eggs, beaten

1/2 teaspoon salt

1/4 teaspoon pepper

Sprinkle the zucchini, tomato, onion and cheese into a greased 10-inch quiche dish. Beat the milk, baking mix, eggs, salt and pepper in a bowl until smooth. Pour over the vegetables. Bake at 400 degrees for 15 minutes or until a knife inserted near the center comes out clean.

Yield: 6 servings.

Angel Hair Pasta Primavera

1 (16-ounce) package angel hair pasta

1/2 cup fresh green peas

1/2 cup tiny green beans

1/2 cup sliced mushrooms

1/2 cup chopped fresh asparagus

1/4 cup butter

1 cup light cream

Freshly ground pepper

Grated Parmesan cheese

Cook the pasta using the package directions; drain. Sauté the peas, beans, mushrooms and asparagus in the butter in a saucepan until tender-crisp. Add the cream and pepper. Simmer until the sauce is slightly thickened. Pour over the pasta and toss to coat. Sprinkle with the Parmesan cheese.

Yield: 6 servings.

Rigatoni-Broccoli Bake

16 ounces rigatoni

2 quarts boiling water

1 tablespoon vegetable oil

2 teaspoons salt 1/3 cup margarine

1/3 cup flour 3 cups milk

3/4 cup grated Parmesan cheese

1/2 teaspoon garlic salt

1/8 teaspoon each nutmeg and thyme

1 1/2 cups shredded Cheddar cheese

1 1/2 pounds fresh broccoli florets

3/4 cup shredded Swiss cheese

Cook the rigatoni in the boiling water with the oil and salt in a large saucepan using the package directions. Melt the margarine in a saucepan. Blend in the flour; add the milk. Cook over low heat until smooth and thickened, stirring constantly. Add the Parmesan cheese, garlic salt, nutmeg, thyme and Cheddar cheese; mix well. Pour over the cooked rigatoni. Cook the broccoli in a vegetable steamer or a small amount of water in a saucepan for 5 minutes or until tender-crisp. Add to the rigatoni. Spoon into a greased 9x13-inch baking dish; sprinkle with the Swiss cheese. Bake at 350 degrees for 20 minutes.

Yield: 8 servings.

Penne Pasta with Spinach and Almonds

8 ounces uncooked penne

2 teaspoons salt

2 tablespoons sliced almonds

1 teaspoon olive oil

1 clove of garlic, minced

1 pound spinach, coarsely chopped

3 tablespoons golden raisins

½ teaspoon vegetable bouillon granules

2 medium plum tomatoes, peeled, seeded, chopped

3 tablespoons grated Parmesan cheese

Cook the pasta with the salt in a saucepan using the package directions. Toast the almonds in a nonstick 12-inch skillet over low heat until golden brown, stirring and shaking frequently. Remove from the skillet. Add the olive oil and garlic to the skillet. Sauté until the garlic is golden brown. Increase the heat to medium-high. Add the spinach, raisins and bouillon granules. Cook just until the spinach wilts. Combine the pasta, spinach mixture and tomatoes in a saucepan. Cook until heated through. Add 2 tablespoons of the Parmesan cheese and toss to mix well. Spoon into a serving bowl. Top with the almonds and remaining Parmesan cheese.

Yield: 4 servings.

Oriental Linguini

1 pound fresh linguini, or 12 ounces dried linguini

¼ cup oriental sesame oil

3 tablespoons soy sauce

¼ teaspoon freshly ground black pepper

¼ cup chopped watercress leaves

¼ cup finely chopped red bell pepper

1 small clove of garlic, minced

Cook the linguini using the package directions; drain. Combine the sesame oil, soy sauce and pepper in a large bowl. Add the linguini to the oil mixture and toss. Add the watercress, bell pepper and garlic and toss until mixed.

Yield: 4 servings.

Noodles with Thai Peanut Sauce

1 cup thinly sliced carrots

1 cup thinly sliced bell peppers

1 cup thinly sliced zucchini

3 cloves of garlic, minced

1 1/2 teaspoons minced fresh ginger

7 tablespoons tamari sauce (or soy sauce)

6 tablespoons creamy peanut butter

1/4 cup rice vinegar

1/4 cup honey

1 teaspoon roasted (dark) sesame oil

16 ounces thin spaghetti or oriental noodles, cooked

1/2 to 3/4 cup minced green onions

Sauté the carrots, green peppers and zucchini in a skillet until tender-crisp. Combine the garlic, ginger, tamari sauce, peanut butter, rice vinegar, honey and sesame oil in a blender container; process until well mixed. Place the hot noodles in a large bowl. Add the sauce; toss until coated. Add the green onions and sautéed vegetables; toss to mix.

Yield: 8 servings.

Neapolitan Tomato Sauce with Pasta

1 to 1 1/2 pounds fresh tomatoes, peeled, seeded, chopped

1 clove of garlic, minced

1/4 teaspoon sugar

Salt and freshly ground pepper to taste

3 tablespoons olive oil

1 tablespoon finely chopped fresh basil

12 ounces spaghetti

Combine the tomatoes, garlic, sugar, salt, pepper and olive oil in a large saucepan. Cook over medium heat for 20 minutes, stirring occasionally. Stir in the basil. Adjust the seasonings. Cook the spaghetti using the package directions; drain. Add the spaghetti to the tomato sauce, tossing gently to coat. Spoon into a serving dish.

Yield: 4 servings.

Tortellini with Fresh Pesto Sauce

1 (12-ounce) package cheese tortellini

1 cup Pesto Sauce

1 tomato, peeled, seeded, chopped

1 zucchini, chopped

2 green onions, chopped

1 (4-ounce) package mozzarella string cheese, chopped

3 tablespoons pine nuts

4 ounces black olives, halved

Salt and pepper to taste

Cook the cheese tortellini using the package directions; drain. Toss all the ingredients together. Serve warm or chilled.

Yield: 6 servings.

Pesto Sauce

2 to 3 cups fresh basil leaves

1/2 cup olive oil

2 tablespoons pine nuts

2 to 3 cloves of garlic, minced

1/2 cup grated Parmesan cheese

2 tablespoons grated Romano cheese

3 tablespoons butter, softened

Blend the basil, olive oil, pine nuts and garlic in a food processor. Pour into a bowl and stir in the Parmesan cheese, Romano cheese and butter.

Macaroni and Mustard Cheddar

8 ounces uncooked macaroni

1 teaspoon butter

1 egg, beaten

1 teaspoon salt

1 teaspoon dry mustard

1 tablespoon hot water

1 cup milk

3 cups shredded sharp Cheddar cheese

Cook the macaroni using the package directions; drain. Stir the butter and egg into the hot macaroni. Mix the salt, dry mustard and hot water in a bowl. Add the milk; mix well. Add 2 cups of the cheese to the milk mixture; mix well. Add the macaroni mixture; mix well. Pour into a buttered casserole. Sprinkle with the remaining cheese. Bake at 350 degrees for 45 minutes or until set and the top is crusty.

Yield: 4 servings.

Tortellini and Creamed Spinach

3 (9-ounce) packages frozen creamed spinach, prepared

1/2 cup milk

2 (9-ounce) packages meat tortellini, prepared

1 cup chopped tomato

1/2 teaspoon dried basil

1/2 cup grated Parmesan cheese

Mix the creamed spinach with the milk in a bowl. Spoon half the creamed spinach mixture into a buttered shallow 2 1/2-quart casserole. Top with half the tortellini and chopped tomato. Repeat the layers with the remaining creamed spinach, tortellini and tomato. Sprinkle with the basil and cheese. Bake, covered with foil, at 350 degrees for 40 minutes.

Yield: 6 servings.

desserts
beverages

Desserts • Beverages

Chocolate Fondue

1½ cups semisweet chocolate chips

½ cup heavy cream

½ cup light corn syrup

Vanilla extract to taste

1 tablespoon frozen orange juice concentrate

1 pint strawberries

4 bananas, sliced

1 pineapple, cut into chunks

4 mandarin oranges, cut into chunks

4 kiwifruit, cut into chunks

½ pound cake, cut into chunks

Combine the chocolate chips, cream and corn syrup in a large microwave-safe bowl. Microwave on High for 2½ minutes, stirring twice. Stir in the vanilla and orange juice concentrate. Microwave for 5 minutes longer, stirring 3 times. Pour into a fondue pot. Serve with the fruit and cake.

Yield: 12 servings.

Chocolate Mint Dessert

1 (16-ounce) package Oreo cookies, finely crushed

½ cup margarine

½ gallon vanilla ice cream, softened

½ cup crème de menthe syrup

Combine the cookie crumbs and margarine in a bowl; mix well. Reserve a small amount of the crumb mixture for topping. Press the remaining crumb mixture over the bottom of a greased 9x13-inch dish. Combine the ice cream and crème de menthe syrup in a bowl; mix until blended. Spread over the prepared shell. Sprinkle with the reserved crumb mixture. Freeze until firm. Move to the refrigerator 10 minutes before serving.

Yield: 15 servings.

Quick Jelly Rolls

1 unbaked pie pastry

2 or 3 tablespoons jelly, any flavor

Confectioners' sugar

Place the pie pastry on a nonstick baking sheet. Spread the jelly over the pastry; roll as for a jelly roll. Bake at 400 degrees for 10 to 12 minutes or until light brown. Cool. Slice and sprinkle with the confectioners' sugar.

Yield: 12 servings.

Orange Surprise Tarts

1 (5-ounce) milk chocolate bar

2 tablespoons milk

10 pastry tart shells, baked

3 egg yolks, lightly beaten

1/4 cup orange juice

1 teaspoon lemon juice

1/2 cup sugar

1/8 teaspoon salt

2 cups whipped topping

1 tablespoon grated orange peel

Fresh orange slices

Melt the chocolate in the milk in a double boiler over hot water; stir until smooth. Cool slightly and spread over the bottom of the tart shells. Chill, covered, in the refrigerator. Place the egg yolks in a double boiler; add the orange juice and lemon juice gradually. Stir in the sugar and salt. Cook until thickened, stirring constantly. Cool to room temperature. Fold in the whipped topping and orange peel. Spoon into a large bowl. Chill, covered, until serving time. Spoon into the tart shells just before serving. Garnish with fresh orange slices.

Yield: 10 servings.

Blender Chocolate Mousse

2 cups semisweet chocolate chips, melted
1/2 cup sugar
3/4 cup pasteurized egg substitute
1 cup hot milk
2 teaspoons brandy extract
Whipped cream

Combine the chocolate, sugar and egg substitute in a blender container. Add the hot milk and brandy extract. Process on medium speed until smooth. Pour into dessert dishes. Chill for 1 hour. Garnish with the whipped cream.

Yield: 6 servings.

Sweet Dream Dessert

1 envelope Knox unflavored gelatin
1/4 cup cold skim milk
1/2 cup skim milk
1 cup low-fat ricotta cheese
1 cup low-fat cottage cheese
1/2 cup sugar
1 teaspoon vanilla extract
1/2 cup thawed frozen strawberries
1/4 cup miniature semisweet chocolate chips
Pirouette cookies

Sprinkle the gelatin over 1/4 cup cold milk in a blender container. Let stand for 2 minutes. Bring 1/2 cup milk to a boil in a saucepan. Add to the gelatin. Process at low speed for 2 minutes or until the gelatin is completely dissolved. Add the ricotta cheese, cottage cheese, sugar and vanilla. Process at high speed for 2 minutes or until well blended. Pour equal amounts into 2 bowls. Purée the strawberries in the blender, straining if desired. Stir into 1 bowl of pudding. Chill both bowls of pudding for 3 hours or until set. Whisk until smooth. Stir the chocolate chips into the plain pudding. Spoon the pudding mixtures side-by-side into 6 dessert bowls. Serve with pirouette cookies.

Yield: 6 servings.

Photograph for this recipe is on page 104.

Chocolate Brownie Trifle

1 (22-ounce) package fudge brownie mix

$\frac{1}{4}$ cup chocolate syrup

1 (4-ounce) package chocolate fudge instant pudding mix

1 package fun-size Heath bars, crushed

12 ounces whipped topping

Prepare and bake the brownies using the package directions. Prick the top of the warm brownies at 1-inch intervals. Brush with the chocolate syrup. Cool. Crumble into bite-size pieces. Prepare the pudding using the package directions. Layer the brownie pieces, pudding, crushed candy and whipped topping $\frac{1}{2}$ at a time in a 3-quart trifle bowl. Chill for 8 hours or longer.

Yield: 16 servings.

Olde English Raspberry Trifle

4 trifle sponge cakes or 1 pound cake, sliced

Raspberry jam

$\frac{1}{2}$ cup orange juice

2 cups raspberries

$1\frac{1}{2}$ cups milk

3 eggs

$\frac{1}{4}$ cup sugar

$\frac{1}{2}$ cup plus 2 tablespoons heavy cream, whipped

$\frac{1}{8}$ cup chopped nuts

Spread the cake slices with the jam. Place 2 slices together, sandwich fashion. Repeat until all the slices are used. Arrange in a glass serving bowl. Sprinkle with the orange juice. Reserve $\frac{1}{2}$ cup raspberries. Sprinkle the remaining raspberries over the cake. Heat the milk in a saucepan almost to boiling. Whisk the eggs and sugar in a bowl. Stir into the hot milk. Cook until the custard is thickened and coats the back of a wooden spoon, stirring constantly. Let cool. Spoon over the raspberries. Chill until set. Pipe the whipped cream over the custard. Garnish with the nuts and reserved raspberries.

Yield: 8 servings.

Flan

6 eggs
2 (5-ounce) cans evaporated milk
1 cup sugar
Salt to taste
1 tablespoon vanilla extract
1 cup sugar
1 teaspoon water

Beat the eggs in a mixer bowl until frothy. Add the evaporated milk, 1 cup sugar, salt and vanilla; mix well. Combine 1 cup sugar and the water in a nonstick skillet over medium-low heat. Cook over low heat until the sugar melts and turns light brown, shaking pan occasionally and stirring frequently. Pour the caramelized sugar into a greased 10-inch baking pan, tilting the pan to coat evenly. Spoon the filling carefully into the baking pan. Place in a large pan of boiling water. Bake at 350 degrees for 1 to 1½ hours or until set. Cool on a wire rack. Chill in the refrigerator. Invert onto a serving plate to serve.

Yield: 10 servings.

Marshmallow Custard

2 eggs
2 tablespoons sugar
2 cups half-and-half
½ teaspoon vanilla extract
6 large marshmallows

Beat the eggs lightly in a bowl. Add the sugar, half-and-half and vanilla; mix well. Place 1 marshmallow in the bottom of each of 6 custard cups. Pour the custard mixture over the marshmallows, dividing equally. Place the custard cups in a pan of hot water. Bake at 325 degrees for 40 minutes or until a knife inserted in the custard comes out clean. Let cool in the refrigerator.

Yield: 6 servings.

Bavarian Mint Tarts

15 single saltine crackers, crushed
3 egg whites, stiffly beaten
1 cup chopped nuts
1 cup sugar
1 teaspoon vanilla extract
1½ cups softened margarine
3 cups confectioners' sugar
6 ounces semisweet chocolate, melted
1½ cups pasteurized egg substitute
1½ teaspoons peppermint flavoring
1 teaspoon vanilla extract Whipped cream
Peppermint candy or candy canes, crushed

Combine the crackers, egg whites, nuts, sugar and vanilla in a bowl; mix well. Spoon into foil-lined muffin cups. Bake at 325 degrees for 14 minutes. Cream the margarine in a mixer bowl. Add the confectioners' sugar gradually; beat for 5 minutes. Add the cooled chocolate; beat for 3 minutes. Beat in the egg substitute ¼ cup at a time. Add the peppermint flavoring and 1 teaspoon vanilla; beat for 5 minutes. Fill the muffin cup liners to the top. Freeze until firm. Move to the refrigerator 10 minutes before serving. Top with whipped cream and crushed candy.

Yield: 24 servings.

Biscuit Tortoni

1 cup crushed almond macaroon cookies
⅓ cup chopped toasted almonds
3 tablespoons melted butter
1 teaspoon almond extract
3 pints vanilla ice cream, slightly softened
1 (12-ounce) jar apricot preserves

Line 6 muffin cups with paper liners. Mix the cookies, almonds, butter and almond extract in a bowl. Reserve ¼ cup of the mixture for topping. Sprinkle half the remaining mixture in the prepared muffin cups. Spoon half the ice cream over the crumbs. Drizzle with half the preserves and sprinkle with the remaining crumb mixture. Repeat the ice cream and preserve layers; top with the reserved crumbs. Freeze, covered, for 1 hour or until 10 minutes before serving. Let stand at room temperature for 10 minutes to soften slightly.

Yield: 6 servings.

Frango Mint Bombe

1 cup butter, softened

1 cup confectioners' sugar

2 cups semisweet chocolate chips, melted

1 to 1½ cups pasteurized egg substitute

½ teaspoon peppermint extract

Toasted almonds or chocolate sprinkles

Cream the butter and confectioners' sugar in a mixer bowl until light and fluffy. Add the melted chocolate chips; mix well. Beat in the egg substitute. Add the peppermint extract and mix well. Spoon 2 heaping tablespoons of the chocolate mixture into paper-lined muffin cups. Top with toasted almonds. Freeze for 2 to 3 hours. Move to the refrigerator 30 minutes before serving.

Yield: 16 servings.

Chocolate Cake

1¼ cups flour

½ cup baking cocoa

¼ cup cornstarch

1 teaspoon baking powder

½ teaspoon baking soda

½ teaspoon salt

1¼ cups sugar

1 cup water

½ cup dark corn syrup

3 egg whites, stiffly beaten

Confectioners' sugar

Mix the flour, baking cocoa, cornstarch, baking powder, baking soda and salt together. Combine the sugar, water and corn syrup in a mixer bowl; mix well. Add the dry ingredients, beating well. Pour into a bundt pan sprayed with nonstick cooking spray. Bake at 350 degrees for 35 to 40 minutes or until the cake tests done. Let cool in the pan for 5 minutes. Remove to a serving plate. Dust with confectioners' sugar.

Yield: 16 servings.

Chocolate-Cherry Cake Ring

2 cups flour
3/4 cup sugar
1 teaspoon baking soda
1 teaspoon cinnamon
1/8 teaspoon salt
2 eggs, beaten
1/2 cup vegetable oil
2 teaspoons vanilla extract
1 (21-ounce) can cherry pie filling
1 cup semisweet chocolate chips
1 cup chopped walnuts
Confectioners' sugar to taste

Sift the flour, sugar, baking soda, cinnamon and salt together. Combine the eggs, oil and vanilla in a mixer bowl; beat until blended. Add the flour mixture; beat well. Stir in the pie filling, chocolate chips and walnuts. Pour into a greased and floured 10-inch fluted tube pan. Bake at 350 degrees for 1 hour or until the cake tests done. Let cool in the pan for 10 minutes. Invert onto a serving plate. Sprinkle with the confectioners' sugar.

Yield: 16 servings.

Chocolate Pound Cake

3 cups sifted flour
1/2 cup baking cocoa
1/2 teaspoon baking powder
1/2 teaspoon salt
1 cup butter, softened
1/2 cup shortening
3 cups sugar
5 eggs
1 cup milk
2 teaspoons vanilla extract

Mix the flour, baking cocoa, baking powder and salt together. Cream the butter, shortening and sugar in a mixer bowl until light and fluffy. Add the eggs and milk alternately with the flour mixture, mixing well after each addition. Stir in the vanilla. Spoon into a nonstick tube or bundt pan. Bake at 325 degrees for 1 hour and 25 minutes or until the cake tests done.

Yield: 16 servings.

Sour Cream Pound Cake

1 cup sour cream

1 cup margarine, softened

3 cups sugar

6 eggs

3 cups flour

1/4 teaspoon baking soda

1 teaspoon vanilla extract

Beat the sour cream, margarine and sugar in a large mixer bowl until smooth. Beat in the eggs 1 at a time. Add the flour, baking soda and vanilla; mix well. Spoon into a greased and floured bundt or tube pan. Bake at 325 degrees for 1 hour and 10 minutes or until the cake tests done.

Yield: 16 servings.

Orange Pecan Cake

1 cup butter or margarine, softened

1 cup sugar   3 egg yolks

1 tablespoon orange juice

2 cups flour   1 teaspoon baking powder

1 teaspoon baking soda

1 1/4 cups sour cream

Grated peel of 1 orange

1 cup chopped pecans, toasted

3 egg whites, stiffly beaten

1/2 cup sugar   1 1/3 cups orange juice

1/2 cup slivered almonds

Cream the butter and 1 cup sugar in a mixer bowl until light and fluffy. Beat in the egg yolks 1 at a time. Beat in 1 tablespoon orange juice. Add a sifted mixture of the flour, baking powder and baking soda alternately with the sour cream, beating well after each addition. Stir in the orange peel and pecans. Fold in the egg whites. Spoon into a greased 10-cup bundt pan. Bake at 350 degrees for 50 minutes or until the cake tests done. Cool in the pan for 10 minutes. Invert onto a serving platter. Drizzle with a mixture of 1/2 cup sugar and 1 1/3 cups orange juice just before serving. Sprinkle with the almonds.

Yield: 16 servings.

Gateau au Chocolat

4 ounces sweet chocolate

1/2 cup butter, softened

4 egg whites, at room temperature

4 egg yolks

4 teaspoons sugar

4 teaspoons flour

Confectioners' sugar

Chocolate curls

Preheat the oven to 425 degrees. Melt the chocolate in a double boiler, stirring occasionally. Remove from the heat. Stir in the butter. Beat the egg whites in a mixer bowl until stiff peaks form. Beat the egg yolks until thickened and light yellow. Add the sugar gradually, beating constantly. Add the flour gradually; mix well. Blend into the chocolate mixture. Fold into the stiffly beaten egg whites gently. Spoon into a lightly greased and waxed-paper-lined 5x9-inch loaf pan. Place the pan in the oven. Reduce the oven temperature to 350 degrees. Bake at 350 degrees for 25 minutes. Cool in the pan on a wire rack. Chill for 4 hours or longer. Loosen from the sides of the pan. Invert onto a serving plate. Dust with confectioners' sugar. Garnish with chocolate curls. Cut into 3/4-inch slices.

Yield: 10 servings.

Graham Cracker Sponge Cake

6 egg yolks

1 cup sugar

1 teaspoon vanilla extract

1/2 teaspoon almond extract

1 cup graham cracker crumbs

6 egg whites, stiffly beaten

Beat the egg yolks and sugar in a mixer bowl until smooth. Add the flavorings; mix well. Stir in the graham cracker crumbs. Fold in the egg whites. Spoon into an ungreased nonstick 10-inch tube pan. Bake at 350 degrees for 40 to 50 minutes or until the cake tests done. Invert on the funnel to cool completely. Loosen the cake from the side of the pan. Invert onto a cake plate.

Yield: 10 servings.

Cheesecake Squares

1/3 cup margarine, softened

1/3 cup packed brown sugar

1 cup flour

1/2 cup finely chopped walnuts

8 ounces cream cheese, softened

1/4 cup sugar

1 egg

2 tablespoons milk

1 tablespoon lemon juice

1/2 teaspoon vanilla extract

Cream the margarine and brown sugar in a bowl with a fork until light and fluffy. Add the flour, mixing until crumbly. Stir in the walnuts. Reserve 1 cup of the crumb mixture. Press the remaining crumb mixture over the bottom of an 8x8-inch baking dish. Beat the cream cheese, sugar, egg, milk, lemon juice and vanilla in a mixer bowl until smooth. Spread over the prepared layer; sprinkle with the reserved crumb mixture. Bake at 350 degrees for 12 to 15 minutes or until brown. Let stand until cool. Cut into squares.

Yield: 24 servings.

Overnight Caramel Strata

1 cup packed dark brown sugar

1/2 cup unsalted butter

2 tablespoons light corn syrup

12 slices white bread

6 eggs

1 1/2 cups milk

1 teaspoon vanilla extract

1/4 teaspoon salt

Combine the brown sugar, butter and corn syrup in a small heavy saucepan. Cook over medium-low heat until the brown sugar dissolves and the butter melts, stirring to mix well. Spread evenly in a buttered 9x13-inch baking dish. Trim the crusts from the bread. Arrange 6 slices in a single layer in the prepared dish. Top with the remaining bread, trimming to fit if needed. Whisk the eggs, milk, vanilla and salt in a bowl until blended. Pour over the bread. Chill, covered, overnight. Bake at 350 degrees for 40 minutes or until puffed and golden brown. Let stand for 5 minutes before serving. Cut into servings. Invert onto serving plates.

Yield: 12 servings.

PEACH MELBA

1½ cups milk 1 cup flour 2 eggs

2 tablespoons sugar ⅛ teaspoon salt

1 tablespoon vegetable oil or melted butter

32 ounces ice cream, softened

Melba Sauce 16 peach slices

Whipped cream

Combine the first 6 ingredients in a bowl. Beat with a wire whisk until blended. Place 2 tablespoons of the batter in a lightly greased 6-inch skillet over medium heat. Lift and tilt the skillet to spread the batter. Return to the heat. Brown on 1 side. Invert onto a paper towel. Repeat to make 16 crêpes, greasing the skillet occasionally. Place crêpes on a work surface. Scoop 2 ounces ice cream onto each crêpe; roll to enclose. Top with Melba Sauce, a peach slice and whipped cream.

Yield: 16 servings.

MELBA SAUCE

1 cup frozen raspberries 1 teaspoon sugar

1 teaspoon cornstarch ½ cup currant jelly

Thaw the raspberries. Mix all the ingredients in a saucepan. Cook over low heat until the syrup is clear. Strain through a sieve; cool. Store, covered, in the refrigerator.

SOUTHERN AMBROSIA

Sections of 10 large seedless oranges, drained

1 (20-ounce) can crushed pineapple, drained

1 (14-ounce) package frozen grated coconut, thawed, or 4 cups freshly shredded coconut

Combine the oranges, pineapple and coconut in a bowl; mix well. Chill for up to 24 hours. Serve from a clear glass or crystal bowl or in individual dessert dishes.

Yield: 12 servings.

Poached Pears in Red Currant Jelly

4 large Anjou or Bartlett pears

$1\frac{1}{2}$ cups red currant jelly

$\frac{1}{3}$ cup sugar

2 to 3 strips lemon peel

3 tablespoons lemon juice

3 or 4 drops of red food coloring

Peel and seed the pears, leaving the pears whole and the stems on. Combine the jelly, sugar, lemon peel and lemon juice in a saucepan. Cook over medium heat until the jelly melts, stirring frequently. Add the pears. Simmer, covered, for 25 minutes, turning the pears frequently. Add the food coloring during the last few minutes of the cooking time. Adjust the cooking time according to the softness or hardness of the pears. Place each pear in a deep individual serving dish. Add the sauce. Chill in the refrigerator. The sauce will thicken as the pears chill.

Yield: 4 servings.

Chocolate Raspberry Meringue

4 egg whites

Dash of salt

$1\frac{1}{2}$ cups sugar

$\frac{1}{4}$ cup baking cocoa

1 teaspoon vanilla extract

$\frac{1}{2}$ cup finely ground hazelnuts or almonds

1 cup heavy cream, whipped

2 cups fresh raspberries

Grease two 8-inch cake pans; line with baking parchment. Beat the egg whites with the salt in a mixer bowl until stiff peaks form. Add the sugar gradually, beating until very stiff. Sift the baking cocoa over the mixture and fold in gently. Fold in the vanilla and hazelnuts. Spoon into the prepared pans. Bake at 350 degrees for 45 minutes. Cool in the pans for 10 minutes; invert onto a wire rack to cool completely. Place 1 meringue on a serving plate. Spread with half the whipped cream and half the raspberries. Top with the remaining meringue. Top with the remaining whipped cream and raspberries.

Yield: 8 servings.

Marshmallow Berry Delight

1½ teaspoons margarine, softened

1 quart fresh, frozen or canned boysenberries or loganberries

3 tablespoons cornstarch 1 cup sugar

4 ounces graham crackers, crushed

½ cup margarine, softened ¼ cup sugar

8 ounces marshmallows 1 cup milk

1 to 2 cups heavy cream, whipped

Grease the sides and bottom of a 9x13-inch dish with 1½ teaspoons margarine. Combine the boysenberries with a mixture of the cornstarch and 1 cup sugar in a saucepan; mix well. Cook over low heat until thickened, stirring frequently. Reserve ½ cup of the graham cracker crumbs. Combine the remaining graham cracker crumbs with ½ cup margarine and ¼ cup sugar; mix well. Press the mixture over the bottom of the prepared dish. Combine the marshmallows and milk in a saucepan. Cook over low heat until the marshmallows melt, stirring constantly. Let stand until cool. Fold in the whipped cream. Spread ½ of the marshmallow mixture over the graham cracker crust. Layer with the berry mixture and remaining marshmallow mixture. Sprinkle with the reserved crumbs. Chill until serving time.

Yield: 15 servings.

Classic Lemon Charlotte

16 to 20 ladyfingers

1 envelope unflavored gelatin

½ cup fresh lemon juice

4 egg yolks, beaten

½ cup sugar ¼ teaspoon salt

1 teaspoon grated lemon peel 4 egg whites

½ cup sugar 1 cup heavy cream, whipped

Lemon peel curls or fresh mint

Split the ladyfingers into halves lengthwise. Trim ½ inch from 1 end of each ladyfinger. Line the bottom and side of a springform pan with ladyfingers, placing rounded sides against the side of the pan and arranging trimmings on the bottom. Soften the gelatin in the lemon juice. Combine the egg yolks, ½ cup sugar and salt in the top of a double boiler. Stir in the gelatin mixture gradually. Cook for 4 minutes or until the mixture begins to thicken, stirring constantly. Remove from the heat. Stir in the lemon peel. Pour into a bowl. Place the bowl in a larger bowl filled with ice. Stir for 5 minutes or until thickened. Beat the egg whites in a mixer bowl until foamy. Add ½ cup sugar gradually, beating until soft peaks form. Fold the egg whites and whipped cream into the lemon mixture. Pour into the prepared pan. Chill, covered, for 6 to 8 hours. Remove the side of the pan carefully. Garnish with lemon peel curls or fresh mint. Chill until serving time.

Yield: 10 servings.

LEMON MERINGUE DESSERT

1/2 cup melted margarine
1 (2-layer) package yellow cake mix
1 egg   1 1/3 cups sugar
1/2 cup cornstarch
Salt to taste   1 3/4 cups water
4 egg yolks, lightly beaten
2 tablespoons margarine
2 tablespoons grated lemon peel
1/2 cup lemon juice   4 egg whites
1/4 teaspoon cream of tartar   1/2 cup sugar

Combine 1/2 cup margarine, cake mix and 1 egg in a bowl and mix well. Press the mixture over the bottom of a greased 9x13-inch baking dish. Combine 1 1/3 cups sugar, cornstarch and salt in a medium saucepan. Stir in the water. Bring the mixture to a boil over medium heat, stirring constantly. Stir a small amount of the hot mixture into the egg yolks. Stir the egg yolks into the hot mixture. Cook until thickened, stirring constantly. Stir in 2 tablespoons margarine, lemon peel and lemon juice. Pour into the prepared pan. Beat the egg whites and cream of tartar in a small mixer bowl until soft peaks form. Add 1/2 cup sugar, beating until stiff peaks form. Spread over the lemon mixture. Bake at 350 degrees for 25 minutes or until the cake tests done. Let stand to cool for 1 hour. Chill, covered, for 1 hour before serving.

Yield: 15 servings.

STRAWBERRY CREAM PIE

1 (3-ounce) package vanilla instant pudding mix
1 cup sour cream
1/4 cup milk
2 teaspoons grated orange or lemon peel
3 1/2 cups whipped topping
1 graham cracker pie shell
1 pint strawberries

Combine the pudding mix, sour cream, milk, orange peel and whipped topping in a bowl. Beat with a whisk until well blended. Spoon half the pudding into the pie shell. Arrange the strawberries over the pudding. Spoon the remaining pudding over the top. Chill for 3 hours before serving.

Yield: 8 servings.

Mile-High Strawberry Pie

1 (10-ounce) package frozen strawberries, thawed

3/4 cup sugar

2 egg whites, at room temperature

1 tablespoon lemon juice

1/8 teaspoon salt

1/2 cup whipping cream

1/2 teaspoon vanilla extract

1 baked (9-inch) pie shell

Combine the undrained strawberries, sugar, egg whites, lemon juice and salt in a mixer bowl. Beat at medium speed for 15 minutes or until thickened, scraping the bowl occasionally. Beat the whipping cream and vanilla in a mixer bowl until stiff peaks form. Fold into the strawberry mixture. Spoon into the pie shell. Freeze for 8 hours or longer.

Yield: 8 servings.

Lemon Fingers

1 cup butter, softened

2 cups flour

1 cup confectioners' sugar

4 eggs

2 cups sugar

1/4 cup flour

1/2 cup lemon juice

1/2 cup confectioners' sugar

Combine the butter, 2 cups flour and 1 cup confectioners' sugar in a bowl; mix until crumbly. Spread in a greased 9x13-inch baking dish, patting evenly. Bake at 350 degrees for 20 minutes. Beat the eggs in a mixer bowl until frothy. Add the sugar, 1/4 cup flour and lemon juice; mix well. Pour over the baked layer. Bake at 350 degrees for 20 minutes longer. Sprinkle with 1/2 cup confectioners' sugar. Cool. Cut into bars.

Yield: 15 servings.

Raisin Mumbles

2½ cups raisins

½ cup sugar

2 tablespoons cornstarch

¾ cup water

3 tablespoons lemon juice

¾ cup butter

1 cup packed light brown sugar

1¾ cups flour

½ teaspoon salt

½ teaspoon baking soda

1½ cups rolled oats

Combine the raisins, sugar, cornstarch, water and lemon juice in a saucepan. Bring to a boil, stirring occasionally. Combine the butter, brown sugar, flour, salt, baking soda and rolled oats in a bowl and mix until crumbly. Pat half the crumb mixture over the bottom of a greased 8x13-inch baking dish. Pour the raisin mixture evenly over the crumbs. Sprinkle the remaining crumb mixture evenly over the top. Bake at 425 degrees for 15 minutes or until brown. Cool. Cut into bars.

Yield: 15 servings.

Valentine Stained Glass Hearts

½ cup butter or margarine, softened

¾ cup sugar   2 eggs

1 teaspoon vanilla extract

2⅓ cups flour

1 teaspoon baking powder

⅓ cup (about) crushed red hard candy

Cream the butter and sugar in a mixer bowl until light and fluffy. Beat in the eggs 1 at a time. Add the vanilla. Sift the flour and baking powder together. Add to the batter gradually. Chill, covered, for 3 to 12 hours. Roll out the dough ⅛ inch thick on a lightly floured surface. Cut out the cookies using a heart-shaped cookie cutter. Place the cookies on a foil-lined cookie sheet. Cut a small heart-shaped design from the center of each cookie. Fill the cut out section with the crushed candy. Bake at 375 degrees for 7 to 9 minutes or until the cookies are light brown and the candy is melted. Do not overcook. Slide the foil off of the cookie sheet. Loosen the cookies carefully when cool.

Yield: 30 servings.

Photograph for this recipe is on page 103.

Citrus Ice Cream Sauce

1 1/3 cups sugar

1/2 cup sifted flour

1 (12-ounce) can frozen orange juice concentrate, prepared

2 1/4 cups light corn syrup

1 cup fresh lemon juice

Combine the sugar and flour in a saucepan; mix well. Stir in the orange juice and corn syrup. Bring to a boil, stirring constantly. Remove from the heat. Stir in the lemon juice. Cool. Store, covered, in the refrigerator. Serve over vanilla ice cream.

Yield: 75 servings.

Baked Fudge Sauce for Ice Cream

4 eggs

2 cups sugar

1 cup melted margarine

1/2 cup flour

1/2 cup baking cocoa

2 teaspoons vanilla extract

1 cup chopped pecans

Cream the eggs and sugar in a large mixer bowl. Add the margarine; mix well. Add a sifted mixture of the flour and baking cocoa. Stir in the vanilla and pecans. Pour into a greased 9x13-inch baking dish. Place the baking dish in a larger pan of water. Bake at 325 degrees for 1 hour. Spoon into serving bowls while warm. Top with ice cream.

Yield: 20 servings.

Peanut Butter Fudge Sauce

1/2 cup heavy cream

2/3 cup semisweet chocolate chips

2 tablespoons creamy peanut butter

Combine the cream and chocolate chips in a 4-cup glass measure. Microwave on High for 1 to 1 1/2 minutes or until the mixture boils vigorously, stirring 2 or 3 times. Add the peanut butter, stirring until smooth. Microwave for 30 seconds longer. Serve over ice cream, frozen yogurt or strawberries.

Yield: 4 servings.

Apple Cider Sangria

3 cups sparkling apple cider

1/3 cup lime juice

1/2 (6-ounce) can frozen lemonade concentrate

1 tablespoon grenadine syrup

Apple or lime slices

Combine the apple cider, lime juice, lemonade concentrate and grenadine syrup in a pitcher; mix well. Pour over ice in glasses. Garnish with apple or lime slices.

Yield: 6 servings.

Ice Cream Apple Refresher

1 quart apple juice, chilled

1 pint vanilla ice cream

1/2 teaspoon cinnamon

Mix the apple juice, ice cream and cinnamon in a blender container. Blend until frothy. Serve immediately.

Yield: 4 servings.

Cinnamon Mocha Mix

1 cup dry nondairy creamer

1 cup hot cocoa mix

3/4 cup instant coffee

1/2 cup sugar

1/2 teaspoon cinnamon

1/4 teaspoon nutmeg

Combine the creamer, cocoa mix, coffee powder, sugar, cinnamon and nutmeg in a bowl; mix well. Store in an airtight container. Combine 3 to 4 heaping teaspoons of the mocha mix with 1 cup boiling water for each serving.

Yield: 15 servings.

Chocolate Brazilian Ice Cream Float

2 ounces unsweetened chocolate

2 cups milk

1/3 cup sugar

2 cups freshly brewed double-strength coffee

1 pint coffee ice cream

Chocolate curls

Combine the chocolate, milk and sugar in a saucepan. Heat over low heat until the chocolate is melted, stirring constantly. Stir in the coffee. Chill, covered, in the refrigerator. Beat vigorously with a rotary beater until foamy just before serving. Pour into 4 tall glasses. Top with a scoop of ice cream. Garnish with chocolate curls.

Yield: 4 servings.

Sparkling Grape Cooler

1 (12-ounce) can frozen grape juice concentrate

1 (2-liter) bottle lemon-lime soda, chilled

Combine the grape juice concentrate and soda in a pitcher, stirring gently to mix. Pour over ice in glasses. Serve immediately.

Yield: 8 servings.

Mixed Fruit Smoothie

1 cup orange juice

1 cup apple juice

4 frozen strawberries

2 slices pineapple

1 frozen banana

Combine the orange juice, apple juice, strawberries, pineapple and banana in a blender container. Process until smooth and frothy. Serve immediately.

Yield: 4 servings.

Chilled Southern Boiled Custard

2 quarts milk

6 eggs, beaten

1 cup sugar

1 teaspoon vanilla extract

Heat the milk in a double boiler. Beat the eggs and sugar in a mixer bowl until thickened. Stir into the milk. Cook until thickened, stirring constantly. Let stand until cool. Stir in the vanilla. Chill, covered, in the refrigerator.

Yield: 10 servings.

Orange Icy

1 (6-ounce) can frozen orange juice concentrate

1/2 cup cold water

1 cup milk

1/2 teaspoon vanilla extract

1/4 cup sugar

Ice cubes

Process the orange juice concentrate, water, milk, vanilla and sugar in a blender until smooth. Add the ice cubes 1 at a time, processing constantly until the mixture reaches the top of the blender container.

Yield: 8 servings.

Dessert Ideas

- Create a quick dessert with fresh fruit slices, a dollop of sour cream or yogurt, and a sprinkle of brown sugar or flaked coconut.

- Use a vegetable peeler to make chocolate curls.

- Whipped cream will be fluffier and less likely to separate if sweetened with confectioners' sugar instead of granulated sugar.

- Save calories by topping desserts with lightly sweetened nonfat sour cream instead of whipped cream.

- For an easy refreshing dessert, shape scoops of lemon or orange sherbet into balls and roll in flaked coconut; freeze until firm. Serve over sliced strawberries or peaches.

- Make quick dessert sundaes by topping ice cream with mashed fruit, preserves, crushed peppermint, chocolate chips, chopped nuts, or crushed candy bars.

- For a continental dessert, serve a plate of assorted fruits and cheese with individual knives for paring and slicing.

- For an instant pastry bag, fill a small plastic bag with icing, meringue, or whipped cream. Seal the bag, snip off one bottom corner, and squeeze out the contents as needed. Just throw away the bag when your decorating is finished.

- To prepare dipping chocolate, melt 2 teaspoons shortening with every 6 ounces chocolate chips. This makes a firmer coating.

- Make a quick and elegant dessert by pouring 1 to 2 tablespoons crème de menthe syrup over vanilla ice cream.

- Substitute crushed granola for graham cracker crumbs in desserts for a delicious difference.

- For a delicious topping for cobblers and puddings, mix 1 cup sour cream and 1/2 cup brown sugar. Chill for 1 hour or longer and mix well before serving.

- Layer angel food or sponge cake with sliced strawberries or peaches and vanilla yogurt for an easy shortcake.

- Make a quick and easy sauce for ice cream or baked pears by melting chocolate-covered mint patties in the microwave.

- For a quick dessert, fill cantaloupe halves with vanilla ice cream and top with fresh berries.

- For a delicious topping for cobbler and puddings, mix 1 cup sour cream and 1/2 cup brown sugar. Chill for 1 hour or longer and mix well before serving.

Herbs

Use fresh whole herbs when possible. When fresh herbs are not available, use whole dried herbs that can be crushed just while adding. Store herbs in airtight containers away from the heat of the stove. Fresh herbs may be layered between paper towels and dried in the microwave on High for two minutes or until dry.

Basil: Can be chopped and added to cold poultry salads. If the recipe calls for tomatoes or tomato sauce, add a touch of basil to bring out a rich flavor.

Bay leaf: The basis of many French seasonings. It is added to soups, stews, marinades, and stuffings.

Bouquet garni: A bundle of parsley, thyme, and bay leaves tied together and added to stews, soups, or sauces. Other herbs and spices may be added to the basic herbs.

Chervil: One of the traditional fines herbes used in French cooking. (The others are tarragon, parsley, and chives.) It is good in omelets and soups.

Chives: Available fresh, dried, or frozen, it can be substituted for raw onion or shallot in nearly any recipe.

Garlic: One of the oldest herbs in the world, it must be carefully handled. For best results, press or crush the garlic clove.

Marjoram: An aromatic herb of the mint family, it is good in soups, sauces, stuffings, and stews.

Mint: Use this herb fresh, dried, or ground with vegetables, desserts, fruits, jelly, lamb, or tea. Fresh sprigs of mint make attractive aromatic garnishes.

Oregano: A staple, savory herb in Italian, Spanish, Greek, and Mexican cuisines. It is very good in dishes with a tomato foundation, especially in combination with basil.

Parsley: Use this mild herb as fresh sprigs or dried flakes to flavor or garnish almost any dish.

Rosemary: This pungent herb is especially good in poultry and fish dishes, as well as in such accompaniments as stuffings.

Saffron: Use this deep-orange herb, made from the dried stamens of a crocus, sparingly in poultry, seafood, and rice dishes.

Sage: This herb is a perennial favorite with all kinds of poultry and stuffings.

Tarragon: One of the fines herbes. Goes well with all poultry dishes whether hot or cold.

Thyme: Used in combination with bay leaf in soups, stews, and sauces.

Garnishes

■ Beautiful garnishes can elevate a commonplace meal to a special event. Beautiful does not have to mean difficult, however, and the trend is toward the natural. The leaves from celery and carrot can be added to the plate for a green touch. Clusters of fresh grapes, fresh dill or basil, edible flower petals or flowers, and fans made of vegetables and fruits add the needed color and texture.

■ Salads can be enhanced with the addition of capers, carrot curls, chives, julienned prosciutto, kumquats, grated citrus peel, hazelnuts, pine nuts, pistachios, croutons, dried fruits, Chinese noodles, olives, pomegranate seeds, broken tortilla chips, fresh herbs, and edible flowers such as nasturtiums, violets, or roses.

■ Garnish soups with slivered nuts, yogurt, crumbled cheese, fennel seeds, caviar, apple or avocado slices, chopped hard-cooked eggs, croutons, lemon or orange slices or peel, mushroom slices, and chives.

■ At dessert time, instead of just spooning the sauce over the cake or mousse, drizzle it into a decorative pattern on the plate or top of the dessert. Make a feather pattern by piping chocolate in horizontal lines across the top of the dessert and draw a wooden pick through the lines in alternate directions at one-inch intervals. Add a citrus twist or swan or a chocolate leaf or butterfly.

■ Radishes lend themselves easily to garnishes. Cut off the stem end of a round radish for a Radish Mum. Make parallel cuts three quarters of the way through the radish from the stem end; make additional cuts perpendicular to the first cuts. Chill in iced water to open.

■ For a Radish Accordion, cut a thin slice from each end of a long narrow radish. Cut crosswise into thin slices, leaving the bottom intact. Chill the radish in iced water to open.

■ Use a large firm tomato for a Tomato Rose. Working from the bottom, cut the peel in a continuous 1/2-inch strip, zigzagging the knife slightly to give a scalloped effect. Holding the peel skin side down, roll it into a spiral; hold the center in place as you roll. Add fresh herb leaves such as basil to resemble rose leaves.

■ For a Cherry Tomato Rose, cut an X into the stem end of the tomato and peel back the skin partway down the side with a sharp knife to form four petals.

■ To make Green Onion Frills, cut off the root end and most of the stem portion of green onions. Make narrow lengthwise cuts at both ends with a sharp knife to produce a fringe. Chill in iced water until the ends curl.

Equivalents

When the recipe calls for	Use
Baking	
½ cup butter	4 ounces
2 cups butter	1 pound
4 cups all-purpose flour	1 pound
4½ to 5 cups sifted cake flour	1 pound
1 square chocolate	1 ounce
1 cup semisweet chocolate chips	6 ounces
2¼ cups packed brown sugar	1 pound
4 cups confectioners' sugar	1 pound
2 cups granulated sugar	1 pound
Cereal & Bread	
1 cup fine dry bread crumbs	4 to 5 slices
1 cup soft bread crumbs	2 slices
1 cup small bread cubes	2 slices
1 cup fine cracker crumbs	28 saltines
1 cup fine graham cracker crumbs	15 crackers
1 cup vanilla wafer crumbs	22 wafers
1 cup crushed cornflakes	3 cups uncrushed
4 cups cooked macaroni	8 ounces uncooked
3½ cups cooked rice	1 cup uncooked
Dairy	
1 cup shredded cheese	4 ounces
1 cup cottage cheese	8 ounces
1 cup sour cream	8 ounces
1 cup whipped cream	½ cup heavy cream
⅔ cup evaporated milk	1 small can
1⅔ cups evaporated milk	1 (13-ounce) can
Fruit	
4 cups sliced or chopped apples	4 medium
1 cup mashed bananas	3 medium
2½ cups shredded coconut	8 ounces
4 cups cranberries	1 pound
1 cup pitted dates	1 (8-ounce) package

Equivalents

When the recipe calls for	Use
Meats	
4 cups chopped cooked chicken	1 (5-pound) chicken
3 cups chopped cooked meat	1 pound, cooked
2 cups cooked ground meat	1 pound, cooked
Nuts	
1 cup chopped nuts	4 ounces shelled 1 pound unshelled
Vegetables	
2 cups cooked green beans	1/2 pound fresh or 1 (16-ounce) can
2 1/2 cups lima beans or red beans	1 cup diced, cooked
4 cups shredded cabbage	1 pound
1 cup grated carrot	1 large
8 ounces fresh mushrooms	1 (4-ounce) can
1 cup chopped onion	1 large
4 cups sliced or chopped potatoes	4 medium
2 cups canned tomatoes	1 (16-ounce) can

Measurement Equivalents

1 tablespoon = 3 teaspoons
2 tablespoons = 1 ounce
4 tablespoons = 1/4 cup
5 1/3 tablespoons = 1/3 cup
8 tablespoons = 1/2 cup
12 tablespoons = 3/4 cup
16 tablespoons = 1 cup
1 cup = 8 ounces or 1/2 pint
4 cups = 1 quart
4 quarts = 1 gallon

1 (6 1/2- to 8-ounce) can = 1 cup
1 (10 1/2- to 12-ounce) can = 1 1/4 cups
1 (14- to 16-ounce) can = 1 3/4 cups
1 (16- to 17-ounce) can = 2 cups
1 (18- to 20-ounce) can = 2 1/2 cups
1 (29-ounce) can = 3 1/2 cups
1 (46- to 51-ounce) can = 5 3/4 cups
1 (6 1/2- to 7 1/2-pound) can or
Number 10 = 12 to 13 cups

Index

GREAT AMERICAN
OPPORTUNITIES INC.